JavaScript Automation: Streamline Your Development Process

A Comprehensive Guide to Automating Your Workflow with JavaScript

BOOZMAN RICHARD

BOOKER BLUNT

Table of Content

TABLE OF CONTENTS

INTRODUCTION

In today's fast-paced digital landscape, automation has become a crucial component for developers, engineers, and businesses striving to improve efficiency, reduce human error, and scale their operations. The advent of **JavaScript** as a versatile and powerful programming language has made it a go-to choice for automating a wide range of tasks, from simple file operations to complex workflows. **"Mastering JavaScript Automation: A Comprehensive Guide"** is designed to equip you with the tools, techniques, and best practices to harness the power of JavaScript for automating tasks, streamlining your development process, and solving real-world challenges with minimal effort.

Whether you are a beginner eager to explore automation or an experienced developer looking to optimize your workflow, this book provides clear, actionable insights and hands-on examples to help you understand the ins and outs of JavaScript automation. It covers everything from the fundamentals to advanced automation patterns, offering you a complete roadmap to master the art of writing efficient, maintainable, and scalable automation scripts.

Why JavaScript?

JavaScript's ability to run both on the **client-side** (in the browser) and **server-side** (via Node.js) makes it a unique tool for automating workflows in web applications, server infrastructure, and cloud environments. The wide adoption of JavaScript in modern development means that whether you are building a simple script to automate repetitive tasks or designing a full-scale enterprise automation solution, JavaScript offers flexibility, performance, and an extensive ecosystem of libraries and frameworks.

By utilizing JavaScript for automation, you tap into a language that has become a cornerstone of both front-end and back-end development. From automating tasks within web applications, streamlining deployment processes, and integrating with external APIs, to managing cloud services and orchestrating complex workflows, JavaScript stands out as a powerful and efficient tool for automation.

What You Will Learn

This book is designed to take you on a journey from the basics of automation to advanced techniques that will help you tackle even the most complex tasks. We will explore:

1. **Foundational Concepts of Automation**: Starting with an introduction to automation in development, you'll learn the principles behind automating repetitive tasks and workflows, as well as the benefits of doing so.

2. **Building Simple Automation Scripts**: We will dive into the core JavaScript syntax needed to write your first automation script. You will learn how to automate common tasks like file handling, API interactions, and more.

3. **Advanced Automation Patterns**: As the complexity of your automation needs grows, we will introduce advanced design patterns such as the **Factory**, **Observer**, and **Command** patterns, helping you write maintainable and scalable scripts.

4. **Integrating JavaScript with Modern Development Tools**: You will learn how to integrate JavaScript automation with tools like **Webpack**, **Babel**, **ESLint**, **Prettier**, and **Jest** to streamline your development and improve code quality.

5. **Optimizing and Scaling Automation**: As your scripts grow in complexity, it becomes essential to optimize them for better performance. We will cover

best practices for performance tuning, memory management, and tools for profiling JavaScript code.

6. **Leveraging Cloud Services for Automation**: One of the most powerful capabilities of modern JavaScript automation is the ability to integrate with cloud platforms such as **AWS Lambda, Google Cloud Functions**, and **Azure Functions**. This book will guide you through running automation scripts in the cloud and orchestrating tasks across multiple services.

7. **Automating the Development Process**: Learn how to automate essential development workflows like continuous integration (CI), testing, linting, and deployment, ensuring that your code is always ready for production.

8. **Real-World Examples**: Throughout the book, you will encounter real-world examples that show how to implement automation in diverse scenarios, from managing microservices in a distributed system to automating social media posts or even provisioning cloud resources dynamically.

Why Automation Matters

Automation is no longer a luxury; it's a necessity in modern software development. By automating repetitive tasks, you not only free up your time but also reduce the risk of human error, ensure consistency across systems, and scale operations more effectively. With **JavaScript** as your automation tool, you are armed with one of the most widely-used and powerful languages in the world. This book will show you how to leverage JavaScript to increase productivity, streamline your workflows, and bring your automation goals to life.

Who Should Read This Book?

This book is perfect for developers, engineers, and IT professionals who want to dive into the world of automation using **JavaScript**. Whether you're:

- **A beginner** with basic JavaScript knowledge looking to expand your skillset to include automation techniques.
- **An intermediate developer** seeking to understand advanced automation patterns and optimize workflows for large projects.

- **A seasoned engineer** or **DevOps professional** looking to automate cloud services, infrastructure, or CI/CD pipelines.

This guide is designed to be both comprehensive and approachable, offering step-by-step instructions, practical examples, and strategies to enhance your coding productivity and automate essential tasks effectively.

How This Book is Structured

This book is organized to guide you through the world of JavaScript automation, starting with foundational concepts and building up to complex, real-world automation challenges. Each chapter is designed to stand on its own, allowing you to dive into any topic based on your interests and current needs. The chapters are structured as follows:

1. **Introduction to Automation and JavaScript**: Understand the need for automation in modern development and why JavaScript is an ideal tool.
2. **Setting Up Your Environment**: Learn how to set up your development environment for automation, including tools like Node.js and npm.

3. **Automating Basic Tasks with JavaScript**: Write your first automation scripts to handle file operations, simple calculations, and repetitive tasks.

4. **Advanced Automation Patterns**: Dive deeper into design patterns that make complex tasks easier to manage and scale.

5. **Optimizing Automation Scripts for Performance**: Learn how to profile and optimize your scripts to handle larger projects and scale effectively.

6. **Integrating JavaScript Automation with Cloud Services**: Automate workflows in the cloud using AWS Lambda, Google Cloud Functions, or Azure Functions.

7. **Automating Social Media Management**: Learn how to automate tasks such as posting and responding on social media platforms like Twitter.

8. **Automating the Development Process**: Automate code formatting, testing, linting, and other development tasks to improve efficiency.

9. **Scaling Automation for Larger Projects**: Discover best practices for scaling automation in large systems and managing dependencies.

10. **Real-World Examples and Case Studies**: Apply the techniques learned in the book to automate

complex workflows, from deploying microservices to automating data processing.

The Future of Automation

As technology continues to evolve, the role of **automation** in software development will only become more integral. With the rise of **machine learning**, **IoT**, and **cloud computing**, automation will play an even more crucial role in managing complex systems and processes. By mastering JavaScript automation, you are positioning yourself for the future, where the ability to automate and scale systems will set you apart from other developers and engineers.

Let's Get Started

Automation is about making systems smarter, more efficient, and scalable. In **"Mastering JavaScript Automation: A Comprehensive Guide"**, you will learn how to harness the power of JavaScript to automate tasks, optimize workflows, and solve real-world challenges. Each chapter will take you closer to mastering the art of automation, whether you're looking to improve your development process, scale your projects, or integrate cloud-based services into your workflows.

So, let's dive in and unlock the full potential of JavaScript automation together.

CHAPTER 1

INTRODUCTION TO

AUTOMATION AND JAVASCRIPT

Overview of Automation in Development

In the world of software development, **automation** is the process of performing tasks without human intervention. Automation can significantly enhance productivity by taking care of repetitive, time-consuming tasks, allowing developers to focus on more complex and creative problems. With automation, developers can:

- **Improve efficiency**: Automate tasks like testing, deployment, and data processing to speed up the development process.
- **Ensure consistency**: Automating repetitive tasks reduces human error and ensures the results are always reliable.
- **Save time and resources**: Automation eliminates the need for manual execution of common tasks, freeing up time for more critical development work.
- **Scale projects**: As projects grow in complexity, automation helps maintain quality and manageability without increasing the workload.

Automation is not limited to software development; it spans various industries, from manufacturing to digital marketing. In the context of software, however, automation focuses primarily on repetitive tasks such as:

- **Code compilation and minification**: Automatically converting source code into optimized, production-ready code.
- **Testing**: Running unit, integration, and functional tests automatically to ensure code quality.
- **Deployment**: Automatically deploying applications to staging or production environments.
- **Task scheduling**: Automating the execution of recurring tasks, such as database backups or server maintenance.

Why JavaScript is an Ideal Tool for Automating Workflows

JavaScript is one of the most popular programming languages, primarily known for its role in web development. However, its versatility extends beyond the browser. JavaScript's power lies in its:

- **Ubiquity**: JavaScript is available on virtually every platform, including browsers, servers (with Node.js), and desktop applications (using frameworks like Electron).
- **Easy integration with web technologies**: As web applications are increasingly at the core of business

operations, automating tasks like data scraping, browser interactions, and API requests becomes easier with JavaScript.

- **Strong library and tool support**: There are numerous libraries and tools built around JavaScript that streamline automation tasks, such as Puppeteer for browser automation, Cheerio for web scraping, and Node.js for building powerful backend automation systems.

- **Event-driven nature**: JavaScript's asynchronous capabilities (with callbacks, promises, and async/await) make it perfect for handling time-sensitive tasks like automating API requests, scheduling jobs, or handling real-time data.

- **Lightweight and flexible**: JavaScript's non-blocking, lightweight execution model ensures that it can run efficiently even for complex automation workflows, from building deployment pipelines to automating development tasks like file manipulation and testing.

The combination of its flexibility, ease of use, and massive ecosystem of tools makes JavaScript an ideal language for streamlining development workflows, automating manual processes, and integrating with other technologies.

Introduction to Basic Automation Concepts

Before diving into JavaScript-specific automation tools and techniques, it's important to grasp some basic concepts that underpin most automation tasks. These concepts serve as the foundation for creating efficient and maintainable automation scripts:

- **Tasks**: The basic units of automation. A task is a specific job or function that needs to be automated, such as running a script, sending an email, or cleaning up old log files.
- **Automation Scripts**: These are programs or scripts that contain the logic to perform tasks. They are often written in programming languages like JavaScript and executed to automate repetitive or scheduled actions.
- **Scheduling**: Automation often requires tasks to run at specific times or intervals. Scheduling involves setting up a system to trigger tasks at defined intervals (e.g., running a backup every night at midnight) using tools like cron jobs in Unix-based systems or third-party scheduling libraries in JavaScript.
- **Error Handling**: Automation can break or fail due to unforeseen conditions. Error handling is the process of anticipating potential issues and designing automation scripts to handle those errors gracefully, ensuring that tasks don't fail silently or cause additional problems.

- **Logging**: Logging involves keeping a record of what tasks were performed, when, and whether they were successful. Logs help in diagnosing errors, auditing automated processes, and maintaining the integrity of the automation system.

- **Workflows**: In automation, a workflow is a sequence of tasks that are performed in a specific order to achieve a larger goal. Workflows can be as simple as a single task or as complex as an entire development pipeline (e.g., from coding to deployment).

By understanding these basic concepts, you're ready to move forward with learning how to apply them using JavaScript in the coming chapters. JavaScript will serve as a powerful tool to simplify and automate your workflow, saving you time and effort while improving the quality and consistency of your development process.

CHAPTER 2

SETTING UP YOUR ENVIRONMENT

Installing Node.js and npm

Before you can start automating your workflow with JavaScript, you need to set up your development environment. The first step is to install **Node.js** and **npm** (Node Package Manager). Node.js is a runtime that allows you to execute JavaScript code outside of the browser, while npm is a package manager that helps you manage libraries and tools you'll use in your automation projects.

Step 1: Installing Node.js

- **Go to the Node.js website**: Visit nodejs.org.
- **Download the installer**: There are two versions available—**LTS (Long Term Support)** and **Current**. It's recommended to use the LTS version for stability, especially for beginners.
- **Install Node.js**: Once the installer is downloaded, run it and follow the installation prompts. The installer will automatically set up both Node.js and npm on your system.

Step 2: Verifying the installation Once installed, open your terminal (Command Prompt, PowerShell, or a terminal emulator on macOS/Linux) and type the following commands to ensure Node.js and npm are correctly installed:

- Check Node.js version:

```bash
node -v
```

- Check npm version:

```bash
npm -v
```

You should see version numbers displayed for both Node.js and npm. If you encounter any errors, double-check the installation process or consult the official Node.js documentation for troubleshooting.

Setting Up a Text Editor or IDE (Visual Studio Code, etc.)

Now that Node.js and npm are installed, you need a place to write your JavaScript code. While you can use any text editor, **Visual Studio Code (VS Code)** is highly recommended due to its robust support for JavaScript, integration with npm, and a wide range of extensions to enhance your coding experience.

Step 1: Installing Visual Studio Code (VS Code)

- **Go to the VS Code website**: Visit code.visualstudio.com.
- **Download and install**: Download the version suitable for your operating system (Windows, macOS, or Linux) and follow the installation steps.

Step 2: Setting Up VS Code for JavaScript Development Once you've installed VS Code, you'll need to configure it for JavaScript development:

- **Install essential extensions**:
    - **Prettier**: For automatic code formatting.
    - **ESLint**: For JavaScript linting to ensure your code follows best practices and is free of errors.
    - **Live Server**: To quickly preview web pages or scripts by launching a local server.
    - **Node.js**: To enable debugging and interacting with Node.js directly from the editor.

You can install extensions directly within VS Code by opening the Extensions view (click the square icon in the left sidebar) and searching for the extension names.

Step 3: Configuring VS Code To further enhance your workflow, you may want to configure your VS Code settings. Some important settings for JavaScript automation include:

- **Auto Save**: Enable auto-save to automatically save files without manual intervention.
- **Format on Save**: Set VS Code to automatically format your code every time you save it. This can be especially useful for maintaining clean, readable code.
- **Enable IntelliSense**: Ensure IntelliSense is enabled to get real-time suggestions for code completion, syntax checking, and error highlighting.

Basic Configuration for Automation Projects

Once your environment is set up, it's time to configure your first automation project. Setting up a clean and organized project structure is key to managing and maintaining your automation scripts effectively.

Step 1: Create a Project Directory Create a folder for your project where you'll store your automation scripts. It's a good practice to organize your code in directories for clarity. For example, you might create a directory structure like this:

```bash
```

```
/my-automation-project
  /scripts
  /logs
  /config
  /node_modules
  package.json
```

- **scripts**: Store your JavaScript automation scripts here.
- **logs**: Save log files that capture execution details (e.g., success, failure).
- **config**: Store configuration files (e.g., API keys, environment settings).
- **node_modules**: This folder is automatically created when you install dependencies with npm.

Step 2: Initialize Your Project with npm Inside your project directory, open the terminal and run the following command to initialize your Node.js project:

```
bash
```

```
npm init -y
```

This command creates a **package.json** file, which contains metadata about your project, including the project name, version, and dependencies. The -y flag automatically fills in default values, but you can manually edit this file later if needed.

Step 3: Install Necessary Packages JavaScript automation often involves using external libraries. For example, if you plan to automate web scraping, you might want to use **Puppeteer** or **Cheerio**.

To install a package, run the following command in the terminal:

```
bash
```

```
npm install puppeteer
```

This command installs Puppeteer and adds it as a dependency in the **package.json** file. You can install as many packages as needed for your project, and npm will manage them for you.

Step 4: Create Your First Automation Script With your project setup complete, it's time to write your first automation script. Create a file called **automation.js** in the **scripts** directory. Here's a simple example of a script that logs the current date and time:

```
javascript
```

```javascript
// automation.js
const currentDate = new Date();
console.log(`Automation Script Executed on:
${currentDate}`);
```

To run your script, go back to the terminal and type:

25

```bash
```

```
node scripts/automation.js
```

You should see the current date and time printed in the terminal.

By following these steps, you've successfully set up your environment for JavaScript automation. The next chapters will dive deeper into writing specific automation scripts, integrating APIs, and leveraging libraries to automate more complex tasks. But before moving forward, ensure your environment is correctly configured, as it serves as the foundation for all the automation workflows you'll build.

CHAPTER 3

INTRODUCTION TO JAVASCRIPT FUNDAMENTALS

Variables, Data Types, and Basic Operators

In JavaScript, understanding **variables**, **data types**, and **operators** is fundamental to creating any type of script, including automation scripts. These concepts form the building blocks of your JavaScript code.

1. Variables Variables store data that can be referenced and manipulated throughout your program. In JavaScript, you can declare variables using the following keywords:

- `var`: Older way of declaring variables (useful for global scope but generally avoided in modern JavaScript).
- `let`: Declares block-scoped variables, which means they are limited to the block, statement, or expression where they are defined.
- `const`: Declares a block-scoped variable whose value cannot be reassigned after initialization.

Example:

```
javascript

let userName = "Alice"; // A string variable
const birthYear = 1990; // A constant variable,
its value can't be changed
```

2. Data Types JavaScript has several basic data types:

- **String**: Represents a sequence of characters enclosed in single or double quotes.

  ```
  javascript

  let message = "Hello, World!";
  ```

- **Number**: Represents numerical values, both integers and floating-point numbers.

  ```
  javascript

  let age = 25; // Integer
  let price = 19.99; // Floating-point number
  ```

- **Boolean**: Represents true or false values.

  ```
  javascript

  let isAvailable = true;
  ```

- **Null**: Represents the intentional absence of any value or object.

```javascript
let result = null;
```

- **Undefined**: Represents a variable that has been declared but not assigned a value.

```javascript
let someVar;
console.log(someVar); // undefined
```

- **Object**: Represents collections of key-value pairs.

```javascript
let person = {
  name: "John",
  age: 30
};
```

- **Array**: An ordered collection of values.

```javascript
let colors = ["red", "green", "blue"];
```

29

3. Basic Operators JavaScript uses operators to perform operations on variables and values. Some common types of operators include:

- **Arithmetic Operators**: Perform basic arithmetic operations.

  javascript

  ```
  let sum = 5 + 3; // addition
  let difference = 5 - 3; // subtraction
  let product = 5 * 3; // multiplication
  let quotient = 5 / 3; // division
  let remainder = 5 % 3; // modulus
  (remainder)
  ```

- **Comparison Operators**: Compare two values and return a boolean (true or false).

  javascript

  ```
  let isEqual = 5 == 5; // checks if values
  are equal (true)
  let isGreater = 5 > 3; // checks if 5 is
  greater than 3 (true)
  let isNotEqual = 5 !== 3; // checks if 5 is
  not equal to 3 (true)
  ```

- **Logical Operators**: Combine multiple boolean expressions.

```javascript
let isTrue = true && false; // logical AND
(false)
let isEither = true || false; // logical OR
(true)
let isNot = !true; // logical NOT (false)
```

Functions and Control Structures (Loops, Conditionals)

1. Functions Functions are reusable blocks of code that can be executed when called. Functions can take parameters (input) and return values (output).

Declaring a Function:

```javascript
function greet(name) {
  console.log("Hello, " + name);
}

greet("Alice"); // Output: Hello, Alice
```

You can also write **arrow functions** (a more modern syntax):

31

```
javascript


const greet = (name) => {
  console.log("Hello, " + name);
};


greet("Bob"); // Output: Hello, Bob
```

2. Control Structures

- **Conditionals (if, else if, else)** Conditionals allow you to execute code based on whether a certain condition is true or false.

```
javascript


let age = 20;


if (age >= 18) {
  console.log("You are an adult.");
} else {
  console.log("You are a minor.");
}
```

You can also chain multiple conditions using `else if`:

```
javascript


let score = 85;
```

32

```javascript
if (score >= 90) {
  console.log("Grade: A");
} else if (score >= 80) {
  console.log("Grade: B");
} else {
  console.log("Grade: C");
}
```

- **Switch Statement** The `switch` statement is an alternative to `if-else` when you need to compare a single expression to multiple possible values.

javascript

```javascript
let day = "Monday";

switch (day) {
  case "Monday":
    console.log("Start of the week!");
    break;
  case "Friday":
    console.log("Almost weekend!");
    break;
  default:
    console.log("Midweek");
}
```

3. Loops Loops are used to repeat a block of code multiple times. Common loops in JavaScript include `for`, `while`, and `do-while`.

- **For Loop**: Executes a block of code a specific number of times.

javascript

```
for (let i = 0; i < 5; i++) {
  console.log(i); // Outputs numbers from 0 to 4
}
```

- **While Loop**: Executes a block of code as long as the condition is true.

javascript

```
let i = 0;
while (i < 5) {
  console.log(i); // Outputs numbers from 0 to 4
  i++;
}
```

- **Do-While Loop**: Similar to the `while` loop, but guarantees that the code will execute at least once.

javascript

```
let i = 0;
do {
  console.log(i); // Outputs numbers from 0 to 4
  i++;
} while (i < 5);
```

Arrays and Objects in JavaScript

1. Arrays Arrays are ordered collections of items, and you can store multiple values in a single variable. You can access array elements using an index, starting from 0.

Creating an Array:

```
javascript
```

```
let colors = ["red", "green", "blue"];
console.log(colors[0]); // Outputs: red
```

Common Array Methods:

- `.push()`: Adds an element to the end of an array.

  ```
  javascript
  ```

  ```
  colors.push("yellow"); // Adds yellow to
  the array
  ```

- `.pop()`: Removes the last element of an array.

```javascript
```

```javascript
colors.pop(); // Removes yellow
```

- `.shift()`: Removes the first element of an array.

```javascript
```

```javascript
colors.shift(); // Removes "red"
```

- `.unshift()`: Adds an element to the beginning of an array.

```javascript
```

```javascript
colors.unshift("purple");  // Adds  purple
to the beginning
```

2. Objects Objects are collections of key-value pairs, where each key is a string (also known as a property), and the value can be any data type.

Creating an Object:

```javascript
```

```javascript
let person = {
  name: "Alice",
  age: 25,
  greet: function() {
```

```
    console.log("Hello, " + this.name);
  }
};
```

```
console.log(person.name); // Outputs: Alice
person.greet(); // Outputs: Hello, Alice
```

You can also use **dot notation** or **bracket notation** to access object properties:

```
javascript
```

```
console.log(person["age"]); // Outputs: 25
```

Common Object Methods:

- `.keys()`: Returns an array of the object's keys.

  ```
  javascript
  ```

  ```
  let keys = Object.keys(person);
  console.log(keys);  //  Outputs:  ["name",
  "age", "greet"]
  ```

- `.values()`: Returns an array of the object's values.

  ```
  javascript
  ```

  ```
  let values = Object.values(person);
  ```

```
console.log(values); // Outputs: ["Alice",
25, function() {...}]
```

This chapter has introduced you to the core JavaScript concepts that will allow you to create automation scripts, from basic variables and data types to control flow with loops and conditionals. In the next chapters, we'll dive deeper into applying these fundamentals to automate real-world tasks effectively.

CHAPTER 4

AUTOMATING BASIC TASKS WITH JAVASCRIPT

Writing Your First Automation Script

In this section, we'll begin by writing a simple automation script using JavaScript. This script will be the foundation for more complex automation tasks, allowing you to understand how JavaScript can be used to automate repetitive processes.

Let's start by writing a script that performs a basic task, such as **logging the current date and time** every time it's executed. This is a simple automation task, but it's essential to get familiar with how automation scripts are structured.

Step 1: Set Up Your Project Directory

If you haven't already, create a new directory for your project. This can be done via the terminal or your file explorer. Inside the directory, create a file called `automation.js`.

Step 2: Writing the Script

39

Open `automation.js` in your text editor (like VS Code), and write the following script:

```javascript

// automation.js

// Get the current date and time
const currentDate = new Date();

// Log the current date and time to the console
console.log(`Automation Script Executed on: ${currentDate}`);
```

Step 3: Running the Script

To run the script, open your terminal, navigate to the project directory, and run the following command:

```bash

node automation.js
```

This will execute the script, and you should see the current date and time printed in the terminal.

Automating Simple File Operations (Read, Write, Delete)

A common use case for automation is handling files. JavaScript (via Node.js) provides various modules to perform file operations, such as reading, writing, and deleting files. We'll use the built-in **fs (File System)** module to work with files.

1. Reading a File

To read a file, we can use the `fs.readFile()` method. This method reads the contents of a file asynchronously and returns the data.

Example: Create a file called `example.txt` in the project directory with some content, such as:

```kotlin
Hello, this is a text file!
```

Now, create a script to read the contents of this file:

```javascript
// automation.js
const fs = require('fs');

// Read the content of 'example.txt'
```

41

```
fs.readFile('example.txt', 'utf8', (err, data)
=> {
  if (err) {
    console.log('Error reading file:', err);
    return;
  }
  console.log('File content:', data); // Output:
Hello, this is a text file!
});
```

Explanation:

- **fs.readFile()**: This method takes the path to the file
  (example.txt), the encoding (utf8), and a callback
  function. If there's an error (e.g., if the file doesn't exist),
  it will print the error. Otherwise, it will print the content
  of the file.

2. Writing to a File

You can also automate the process of writing to a file using the
fs.writeFile() method. This method writes data to a file, and
if the file doesn't exist, it will be created.

Example:

```javascript

// automation.js
```

```
const fs = require('fs');

// Write content to a file
const content = 'This is the new content written
to the file!';

fs.writeFile('output.txt', content, (err) => {
  if (err) {
    console.log('Error writing file:', err);
    return;
  }
  console.log('File written successfully!');
});
```

Explanation:

- **fs.writeFile()**: This method writes the specified content to output.txt. If the file doesn't exist, it will be created. If it does exist, its contents will be overwritten with the new content.

3. Deleting a File

Sometimes, automation tasks involve cleaning up old or temporary files. You can automate this using fs.unlink() to delete files.

Example:

```javascript
javascript

// automation.js
const fs = require('fs');

// Delete the 'output.txt' file
fs.unlink('output.txt', (err) => {
  if (err) {
    console.log('Error deleting file:', err);
    return;
  }
  console.log('File deleted successfully!');
});
```

Explanation:

- **fs.unlink()**: This method deletes the file specified by the path (output.txt). If there's an error (e.g., the file doesn't exist), it will print the error. Otherwise, it will confirm that the file was deleted.

Creating a Task Runner for Repetitive Tasks

A task runner is an essential part of automating workflows. It allows you to define a series of tasks and execute them in sequence or at specific times. One simple way to create a task runner in JavaScript is by using **npm scripts** or writing a custom automation script that handles tasks sequentially.

44

1. Using npm Scripts for Automation

npm allows you to define custom scripts in the `package.json` file, which can be run using the `npm run` command. This is particularly useful for automating tasks like building projects, testing, or starting servers.

Example:

In your `package.json` file, add the following under the `"scripts"` section:

json

```
{
  "name": "automation-project",
  "version": "1.0.0",
  "scripts": {
    "start": "node automation.js",
    "clean": "rm -rf output.txt"
  }
}
```

- **start**: This script runs the `automation.js` script.
- **clean**: This script deletes the `output.txt` file.

To run the `start` script, execute the following command in the terminal:

45

bash

npm run start

To run the `clean` script, use:

bash

npm run clean

2. Writing a Simple Task Runner

If you prefer to write your own task runner, you can create a script that executes multiple tasks in sequence. Here's an example of a custom task runner that runs a series of file operations (reading, writing, and deleting files):

javascript

```
// taskRunner.js
const fs = require('fs');

// Task 1: Read file content
function readFileTask() {
  fs.readFile('example.txt', 'utf8', (err, data)
=> {
    if (err) {
      console.log('Error reading file:', err);
      return;
    }
```

```
    console.log('File content:', data);
    // Task 2: Write to a file
    writeFileTask();
  });
}


// Task 2: Write to a file
function writeFileTask() {
  const content = 'This is the new content
written by the task runner!';
  fs.writeFile('output.txt', content, (err) => {
    if (err) {
      console.log('Error writing file:', err);
      return;
    }
    console.log('File written successfully!');
    // Task 3: Delete the file
    deleteFileTask();
  });
}


// Task 3: Delete the file
function deleteFileTask() {
  fs.unlink('output.txt', (err) => {
    if (err) {
      console.log('Error deleting file:', err);
      return;
    }
    console.log('File deleted successfully!');
```

```
  });
}


// Run the task runner
readFileTask();
```

Explanation:

- **readFileTask()**: This function reads the content of example.txt.
- **writeFileTask()**: This function writes content to output.txt.
- **deleteFileTask()**: This function deletes the output.txt file.

You can extend this task runner by adding more tasks, chaining them together, or even scheduling them to run at specific intervals.

By now, you've written your first automation script, learned how to handle basic file operations, and created a simple task runner for repetitive tasks. These concepts are the foundation for more advanced automation workflows, which we'll explore in the following chapters.

CHAPTER 5

UNDERSTANDING ASYNCHRONOUS JAVASCRIPT

Callbacks, Promises, and Async/Await

One of the key features of JavaScript is its ability to handle **asynchronous operations**. Asynchronous programming allows JavaScript to perform tasks without blocking the execution of other tasks, making it an ideal choice for automation scripts. In this chapter, we'll explore three important concepts that are crucial for understanding asynchronous JavaScript: **callbacks**, **promises**, and **async/await**.

1. Callbacks

A **callback** is a function that is passed as an argument to another function and is executed once that function completes its task. Callbacks are commonly used for asynchronous operations, such as reading a file or making a network request.

Example:

49

Let's say you want to read a file asynchronously. Instead of waiting for the file to be read before moving on to the next operation, you can provide a callback function that will be executed once the file is read.

```javascript
const fs = require('fs');

// Asynchronous file reading with a callback
fs.readFile('example.txt', 'utf8', (err, data) => {
  if (err) {
    console.log('Error reading file:', err);
    return;
  }
  console.log('File content:', data);
});
```

Explanation:

- The fs.readFile() method takes a **callback function** as its third parameter. This callback is executed once the file has been read. If there's an error (like the file not being found), it is passed to the callback function as the err parameter; otherwise, the file content is passed as data.

While callbacks are effective, they can lead to what is known as **callback hell**—a situation where you have many nested callbacks, making the code difficult to read and maintain.

---

2. Promises

A **promise** is an object that represents the eventual completion (or failure) of an asynchronous operation. Promises provide a cleaner and more manageable way to handle asynchronous operations compared to callbacks.

A promise can be in one of three states:

- **Pending**: The initial state, before the operation completes.
- **Fulfilled**: The operation completed successfully.
- **Rejected**: The operation failed.

Example:

Let's rewrite the previous file reading example using a promise.

```javascript

const fs = require('fs');

// Wrapping file reading in a promise
function readFilePromise() {
```

```
   return new Promise((resolve, reject) => {
      fs.readFile('example.txt',   'utf8',   (err,
data) => {
         if (err) {
            reject('Error reading file');
         } else {
            resolve(data);
         }
      });
   });
}


readFilePromise()
   .then((data) => {
      console.log('File content:', data);
   })
   .catch((err) => {
      console.log(err);
   });
```

Explanation:

- The `readFilePromise()` function wraps the file reading process in a **Promise**. If the file is successfully read, the promise is **resolved** with the file content. If there's an error, the promise is **rejected** with an error message.
- The `.then()` method handles the resolved promise, and `.catch()` handles the rejected promise.

52

Promises offer better error handling and more readable code compared to callbacks. However, for more complex asynchronous tasks, chaining multiple promises can still become cumbersome.

3. Async/Await

Async/await is a modern way to work with asynchronous code in JavaScript. It allows you to write asynchronous code that looks and behaves like synchronous code. `async` functions always return a promise, and the `await` keyword is used to pause execution until the promise is resolved or rejected.

Example:

Let's now rewrite the file reading example using `async/await`:

```javascript
const fs = require('fs').promises;   // Using
promises API for fs module

// Async function to read a file
async function readFileAsync() {
  try {
    const          data          =          await
fs.readFile('example.txt', 'utf8');
    console.log('File content:', data);
  } catch (err) {
```

```
    console.log('Error reading file:', err);
  }
}


readFileAsync();
```

Explanation:

- The function `readFileAsync()` is marked as `async`, meaning it will return a promise.
- Inside the function, the `await` keyword is used before `fs.readFile()`, which pauses the execution until the file is read (or an error occurs). If the operation is successful, it logs the file content; otherwise, it catches and logs the error.

Benefits of Async/Await:

- **Cleaner syntax**: Async/await makes asynchronous code look more like synchronous code, improving readability.
- **Better error handling**: With `try/catch`, errors can be handled more naturally, just like in synchronous code.
- **Easier to maintain**: Async/await avoids the nested callbacks that can make your code messy and difficult to debug.

How Asynchronous JavaScript Improves Automation

Asynchronous JavaScript significantly improves the efficiency of automation scripts by enabling the execution of multiple tasks concurrently. This is particularly useful when dealing with tasks that involve waiting, such as file reading, network requests, or database queries.

Without asynchronous behavior, each task would need to finish before the next one could begin, leading to unnecessary delays. With asynchronous JavaScript, tasks can be performed in parallel, improving speed and reducing idle time.

Example:

Imagine an automation script that fetches data from multiple APIs. Using asynchronous JavaScript, you can send all the requests at once and wait for all of them to complete without blocking the script from doing other tasks in the meantime.

```javascript
const fetch = require('node-fetch');  // Using the node-fetch library to make API requests

// Async function to fetch data from multiple APIs
async function fetchData() {
  try {
```

```
    const            response1            =
fetch('https://api.example1.com/data');
    const            response2            =
fetch('https://api.example2.com/data');
    const            response3            =
fetch('https://api.example3.com/data');

    // Wait for all promises to resolve
    const   [data1,   data2,   data3]   =   await
Promise.all([response1, response2, response3]);

    console.log('API    1    Data:',    await
data1.json());
    console.log('API    2    Data:',    await
data2.json());
    console.log('API    3    Data:',    await
data3.json());
  } catch (err) {
    console.log('Error fetching data:', err);
  }
}


fetchData();
```

Explanation:

- By using `Promise.all()`, we send all the requests
  simultaneously. The `await` keyword ensures that the

script waits for all the requests to resolve before processing the data.

- This approach is much faster than waiting for each API request to finish one by one.

Handling Multiple Tasks Concurrently

One of the biggest advantages of asynchronous JavaScript is the ability to handle multiple tasks concurrently without blocking the main thread of execution. This is especially useful for tasks like:

- **Running parallel HTTP requests** (e.g., to external APIs).
- **Performing multiple file operations** (e.g., reading and writing several files at once).
- **Processing large data sets** (e.g., fetching and manipulating data asynchronously).

Example: Concurrent File Operations

Let's say you need to read multiple files concurrently and then process their contents. Using async/await and `Promise.all()`, you can achieve this efficiently.

```javascript
const fs = require('fs').promises;
```

```
// Async function to read multiple files
concurrently
async function readFiles() {
  try {
    const file1 = fs.readFile('file1.txt',
'utf8');
    const file2 = fs.readFile('file2.txt',
'utf8');
    const file3 = fs.readFile('file3.txt',
'utf8');

    // Wait for all files to be read
    const [data1, data2, data3] = await
Promise.all([file1, file2, file3]);

    console.log('File 1 Content:', data1);
    console.log('File 2 Content:', data2);
    console.log('File 3 Content:', data3);
  } catch (err) {
    console.log('Error reading files:', err);
  }
}

readFiles();
```

Explanation:

- Using `Promise.all()`, the files are read concurrently, and the script waits for all of them to be completed before logging their contents. This is far more efficient than reading the files one by one.

In this chapter, we've covered how **callbacks**, **promises**, and **async/await** are used to handle asynchronous operations in JavaScript. These concepts enable automation scripts to perform multiple tasks concurrently, which is crucial for improving the efficiency and scalability of your workflows. Asynchronous programming is essential when building more advanced automation scripts that need to interact with APIs, handle large datasets, or perform multiple operations in parallel.

CHAPTER 6

AUTOMATING THE COMMAND LINE WITH JAVASCRIPT

Using Node.js for Command-Line Automation

Node.js is not only a runtime for building web applications but also a powerful tool for automating command-line tasks. By leveraging the **command-line interface (CLI)** with Node.js, you can create scripts that perform operations directly from the terminal without the need for a graphical interface.

In this section, we'll explore how to use Node.js to create scripts that automate tasks in the command line, such as file handling, text processing, and system management.

1. Setting Up a Command-Line Script in Node.js

To start automating the command line with Node.js, you'll need to write JavaScript that interacts with the terminal and executes commands. The simplest form of command-line automation with Node.js involves using the `process.argv` array to access command-line arguments.

Example:

javascript

```
// cliScript.js
```

```
// Accessing command-line arguments
const args = process.argv.slice(2); // process.argv includes the node executable path and script path, so we slice the array to get user inputs
console.log("Command-line arguments:", args);
```

To run this script, open your terminal and type:

bash

```
node cliScript.js Hello World
```

Output:

less

```
Command-line arguments: [ 'Hello', 'World' ]
```

This script simply logs the command-line arguments passed to it. This concept forms the basis for more advanced automation tasks, where you might need to pass configurations, filenames, or other parameters.

Implementing Simple CLI Tools with JavaScript

Node.js allows you to build full-fledged **CLI tools** that can automate repetitive tasks, like file manipulation, text processing, or system maintenance. We'll use Node.js's built-in modules, such as `fs` (for file system operations) and `path` (for handling file and directory paths), to create a basic CLI tool that interacts with files and directories.

Example: Creating a Basic CLI Tool to Read and Write Files

Let's build a simple tool that takes a filename as an argument, reads the file, and appends text to it.

1. **Create a script called `fileManipulator.js`:**

javascript

```
const fs = require('fs');
const path = require('path');

// Retrieve the file name and text from command-
line arguments
const fileName = process.argv[2];
const                  textToAppend               =
process.argv.slice(3).join(" ");  // Join  the
remaining arguments as text to append

// Ensure the file name is provided
```

```
if (!fileName) {
  console.log("Please provide a file name.");
  process.exit(1); // Exit the script if no
filename is provided
}


// Resolve the absolute path to the file
const    filePath    =    path.resolve(__dirname,
fileName);


// Read the file content asynchronously
fs.readFile(filePath, 'utf8', (err, data) => {
  if (err) {
    console.error("Error reading file:", err);
    return;
  }


  console.log("Original content of the file:",
data);


  // Append new text to the file
  fs.appendFile(filePath, '\n' + textToAppend,
(err) => {
    if (err) {
      console.error("Error writing to file:",
err);

      return;
    }
```

```
  console.log(`Successfully appended text to
${fileName}`);
  });
});
```

2. **Running the CLI Tool**:

   o Open your terminal and create a file named `example.txt` with some content, like:

```kotlin
Hello, this is the original file content.
```

   o Run the script to append text to the file:

```bash
node fileManipulator.js example.txt "This
is the new content added by the CLI tool."
```

3. **Expected Output**:

```kotlin
Original content of the file: Hello, this is the
original file content.
Successfully appended text to example.txt
```

4. **Check the File**:

o   After running the script, the `example.txt` file will be updated with the new text, and its content will look like this:

```
csharp
```

```
Hello, this is the original file content.
This is the new content added by the CLI
tool.
```

This simple CLI tool demonstrates how you can use Node.js to automate the process of reading from and writing to files directly from the command line.

Working with the fs (File System) and path Modules

Node.js comes with powerful built-in modules like **fs** (file system) and **path** that allow you to interact with files and directories, making it ideal for automating file operations.

1. The `fs` (File System) Module

The `fs` module provides methods for interacting with the file system. You can use it to read, write, delete, and manipulate files and directories.

Common `fs` Methods:

- **fs.readFile()**: Reads the contents of a file.
- **fs.writeFile()**: Writes data to a file (overwrites the file if it exists).
- **fs.appendFile()**: Appends data to a file.
- **fs.unlink()**: Deletes a file.
- **fs.readdir()**: Reads the contents of a directory.

Example: Deleting a File Using fs.unlink()

javascript

```
const fs = require('fs');

// Deleting a file
fs.unlink('example.txt', (err) => {
  if (err) {
    console.error("Error deleting the file:",
err);
    return;
  }
  console.log('File deleted successfully');
});
```

Explanation:

- fs.unlink() deletes the file example.txt from the current directory. If the file doesn't exist or there's an error, the callback function will log the error.

2. The `path` Module

The `path` module helps with handling and transforming file paths. It allows you to work with file and directory paths in a way that's platform-independent, ensuring your code works across different operating systems.

Common `path` Methods:

- **`path.join()`**: Joins multiple path segments into a single path.
- **`path.resolve()`**: Resolves a sequence of paths or path segments into an absolute path.
- **`path.basename()`**: Returns the last part of a path (file or directory name).
- **`path.dirname()`**: Returns the directory name of a path.

Example: Using `path` to Resolve File Paths

```javascript
const path = require('path');

// Resolve an absolute path from a relative path
const filePath = path.resolve(__dirname, 'example.txt');

console.log('Resolved file path:', filePath);
```

Explanation:

- `path.resolve()` creates an absolute path to `example.txt` based on the current directory (`__dirname`), ensuring that the file can be located no matter where the script is executed from.

Putting It All Together: A CLI Tool for File Management

Let's create a more complete automation CLI tool that allows the user to list, create, and delete files from the command line.

```javascript
javascript

const fs = require('fs');
const path = require('path');

// Get user input
const command = process.argv[2];
const fileName = process.argv[3];

const filePath = path.resolve(__dirname, fileName);

// Command to create a file
if (command === 'create') {
  fs.writeFile(filePath, 'New file created by CLI tool!', (err) => {
```

68

```
    if (err) {
      console.error('Error    creating    file:',
err);
      return;
    }
    console.log(`File    ${fileName}    created
successfully!`);
  });
}


// Command to list files in the directory
else if (command === 'list') {
  fs.readdir(__dirname, (err, files) => {
    if (err) {
      console.error('Error  reading  directory:',
err);
      return;
    }
    console.log('Files    in    the    directory:',
files);
  });
}


// Command to delete a file
else if (command === 'delete') {
  fs.unlink(filePath, (err) => {
    if (err) {
      console.error('Error    deleting    file:',
err);
```

```
    return;
  }
    console.log(`File      ${fileName}      deleted
successfully!`);
  });
}


// Invalid command
else {
  console.log('Invalid  command.  Use  "create",
"list", or "delete".');
}
```

Usage Examples:

1. **Creating a File**:

    bash

    ```
    node cliFileManager.js create test.txt
    ```

2. **Listing Files**:

    bash

    ```
    node cliFileManager.js list
    ```

3. **Deleting a File**:

    bash

```
node cliFileManager.js delete test.txt
```

In this chapter, you've learned how to create command-line automation scripts using Node.js. By using the `fs` and `path` modules, you can interact with files and directories, automate repetitive tasks, and create powerful CLI tools that run directly from the terminal. This ability to automate the command line with JavaScript opens up many possibilities for streamlining workflows and improving efficiency in your development process.

CHAPTER 7

WORKING WITH EXTERNAL APIS FOR AUTOMATION

Introduction to REST APIs

A **REST (Representational State Transfer)** API is a popular way for web services to communicate with clients over HTTP. RESTful APIs allow you to interact with external systems and services by sending HTTP requests (such as GET, POST, PUT, and DELETE) and receiving responses, typically in **JSON** or **XML** format.

Key Features of REST APIs:

1. **Stateless**: Each API request is independent and contains all the necessary data. The server does not store any session or state between requests.

2. **Client-Server**: The client and server operate independently. The client sends requests, and the server processes them and sends responses.

3. **Uniform Interface**: REST APIs follow standard conventions, which makes it easier for developers to work with them.

REST APIs are widely used to integrate third-party services, such as social media platforms, weather services, payment gateways, and more, into your applications. By automating interactions with these APIs, you can automate various tasks like posting on social media, fetching live data, and sending notifications.

Common HTTP Methods:

- **GET**: Retrieve data from the server (e.g., getting a list of items).
- **POST**: Send data to the server (e.g., submitting a form or posting a message).
- **PUT**: Update existing data on the server.
- **DELETE**: Delete data on the server.

Fetching Data and Automating API Requests

Node.js provides several methods to interact with REST APIs, but the most common and convenient one is the **fetch** API, which can be used for making HTTP requests. However, in Node.js, you typically use the `node-fetch` library to achieve this.

1. Installing `node-fetch`

First, you need to install the `node-fetch` package to enable HTTP requests:

73

bash

npm install node-fetch

2. Making GET Requests

A **GET request** is used to fetch data from an API. For example, let's fetch data from a public API like **JSONPlaceholder**, a free fake online REST API that you can use for testing and prototyping.

Example: Fetching Posts from JSONPlaceholder

javascript

```javascript
const fetch = require('node-fetch');

// Define the API endpoint
const                url                =
'https://jsonplaceholder.typicode.com/posts';

// Function to fetch data from the API
async function fetchPosts() {
  try {
    const response = await fetch(url);   // Send
the GET request
    const data = await response.json();   // Parse
the response as JSON
```

```
    // Log the fetched data
    console.log('Fetched Posts:', data);
  } catch (error) {
    console.error('Error    fetching    data:',
error);
  }
}


fetchPosts();
```

Explanation:

- **fetch(url)**: Sends a GET request to the specified URL.
- **response.json()**: Parses the JSON response returned by the API.
- The function is wrapped in **async/await** to handle the asynchronous request and ensure that the data is fetched before proceeding.

Real-World Examples: Automating Social Media Posts, Weather Data Fetching

Now that you understand how to fetch data from APIs, let's explore some real-world examples where API requests can be automated.

---

1. Automating Social Media Posts

Social media platforms such as **Twitter**, **Facebook**, and **Instagram** provide APIs that allow you to automate posting content, managing accounts, and interacting with followers.

Example: Automating Twitter Posts Using the Twitter API

To post content on Twitter programmatically, you'll need to use the **Twitter API** and authenticate your application using **OAuth** credentials.

1. **Install the `twitter` package**:

```bash
bash

npm install twitter
```

2. **Set up authentication and send a tweet**:

Here's an example using the `twitter` library to send a tweet:

```javascript
javascript

const Twitter = require('twitter');

// Configure the Twitter client with API
credentials
const client = new Twitter({
```

76

```
consumer_key: 'your-consumer-key',
consumer_secret: 'your-consumer-secret',
access_token_key: 'your-access-token',
access_token_secret:        'your-access-token-
secret',
});


// Function to send a tweet
async function postTweet() {
  try {
    const        tweet        =        await
client.post('statuses/update', { status: 'Hello,
World! #Automation' });
    console.log('Tweet sent:', tweet);
  } catch (error) {
    console.error('Error    posting    tweet:',
error);
  }
}


postTweet();
```

Explanation:

- The `client.post()` method is used to send a POST request to the Twitter API to publish a tweet. The tweet's content is specified in the `status` parameter.
- You need to set up OAuth credentials from your Twitter Developer account to authenticate your API requests.

With this setup, you can automate posting tweets, schedule posts, or interact with followers programmatically.

---

2. Automating Weather Data Fetching

Another common use case for automation is fetching live weather data using APIs. Let's look at an example of how you can automate fetching weather information from an API like **OpenWeatherMap**.

Step 1: Set Up OpenWeatherMap API

Sign up for a free API key at OpenWeatherMap.

Step 2: Fetch Weather Data

Once you have your API key, you can use it to fetch weather data for any city.

```javascript
const fetch = require('node-fetch');

// OpenWeatherMap API endpoint and your API key
const apiKey = 'your-api-key';
const city = 'London';
```

```javascript
const                        url                    =
`https://api.openweathermap.org/data/2.5/weathe
r?q=${city}&appid=${apiKey}&units=metric`;


// Function to fetch weather data
async function fetchWeather() {
  try {
    const response = await fetch(url);
    const data = await response.json();

    if (data.cod === '404') {
      console.log('City not found');
      return;
    }


    // Extracting and displaying the temperature
and weather description
    const temperature = data.main.temp;
    const            weatherDescription           =
data.weather[0].description;
    console.log(`The   weather   in   ${city}   is
${weatherDescription}   with   a   temperature   of
${temperature}°C.`);
  } catch (error) {
    console.error('Error      fetching      weather
data:', error);
  }
}
```

```
fetchWeather();
```

Explanation:

- **url**: The API endpoint URL is dynamically constructed by inserting the city name and API key.
- **response.json()**: Parses the JSON response returned by the API.
- **data.main.temp**: Retrieves the temperature data in Celsius (based on the `units=metric` query parameter).

This script automates the process of fetching weather data for a specified city and displays the result in the terminal. You can extend this functionality by setting up a scheduled task to fetch and log weather updates daily.

---

3. Scheduling API Requests for Automation

You can automate the execution of your API requests using **cron jobs** (on Unix-based systems) or **task schedulers** (on Windows). By setting up a schedule, you can fetch data or post content at regular intervals.

For example, using **node-cron** (a Node.js library), you can automate fetching weather data every hour:

```bash
```

```
npm install node-cron
```

Then, schedule the task:

```
javascript
```

```
const cron = require('node-cron');
const fetchWeather = require('./fetchWeather');
// Import the fetchWeather function from above

// Schedule the weather fetching every hour
cron.schedule('0 * * * *', () => {
  console.log('Fetching weather data...');
  fetchWeather();
});
```

This script will fetch the weather data every hour (the cron expression 0 * * * * means "at the start of every hour").

Conclusion

In this chapter, we've explored how to interact with **REST APIs** using **GET requests** to fetch data, such as social media posts or weather information, and automate these tasks using JavaScript. By leveraging APIs, you can connect to external systems and automate a wide range of operations—from posting content on social media to retrieving real-time data.

81

Whether you're automating daily weather checks, scheduling posts, or integrating with other web services, working with APIs in JavaScript allows you to build powerful and scalable automation workflows.

CHAPTER 8

AUTOMATING WEB SCRAPING WITH JAVASCRIPT

Introduction to Web Scraping

Web scraping is the process of extracting data from websites. It is commonly used to gather large amounts of data from the internet, such as product listings, news articles, or financial data. By automating web scraping, you can efficiently collect data without manually visiting websites and ing information.

Web scraping typically involves three key steps:

1. **Sending an HTTP request** to the website.
2. **Extracting the relevant data** from the web page (often using the page's HTML).
3. **Processing and storing the extracted data** (e.g., saving it to a file or database).

Web scraping is useful in many real-world scenarios, such as:

- **Monitoring product prices** on e-commerce sites.
- **Extracting job listings** from job boards.
- **Gathering news articles** or blog posts for analysis.

- **Compiling market research data**.

While web scraping can be an incredibly powerful tool, it is important to **respect the website's terms of service** and ensure that your scraping activities don't overwhelm their servers.

Using Libraries like Cheerio and Puppeteer for Scraping

JavaScript offers a variety of libraries to simplify web scraping tasks. Two of the most popular libraries are **Cheerio** and **Puppeteer**.

1. Cheerio: A Lightweight Library for Web Scraping

Cheerio is a fast, flexible, and lean implementation of the jQuery library designed for the server. It allows you to parse HTML and traverse/manipulate the document structure using jQuery-style syntax. Cheerio is useful when you need to scrape static pages (i.e., pages where content is not dynamically generated by JavaScript).

Installing Cheerio:

To use Cheerio, you first need to install it via npm:

```bash

npm install cheerio axios
```

- **Cheerio** is used for parsing and manipulating the HTML.
- **Axios** is used to make HTTP requests.

Example: Scraping Product Data Using Cheerio and Axios

Let's scrape product information (e.g., name, price, and description) from an e-commerce site.

javascript

```
const axios = require('axios');
const cheerio = require('cheerio');

// Define the URL of the e-commerce site
const url = 'https://example.com/products';

async function scrapeProducts() {
  try {
    // Fetch the HTML of the page
    const response = await axios.get(url);
    const $ = cheerio.load(response.data);   //
Load the HTML into Cheerio

    // Extract product data using CSS selectors
    $('.product').each((index, element) => {
      const name = $(element).find('.product-
name').text();
      const price = $(element).find('.product-
price').text();
```

85

```
      const            description           =
$(element).find('.product-description').text();


      console.log(`Product ${index + 1}:`);
      console.log(`Name: ${name}`);
      console.log(`Price: ${price}`);
      console.log(`Description:
${description}`);
      console.log('-------------------------
');
    });
  } catch (error) {
    console.error('Error scraping the website:',
error);
  }
}


scrapeProducts();
```

Explanation:

- **Axios** fetches the HTML content of the page.
- **Cheerio** loads the HTML and allows you to use jQuery-like syntax to query and manipulate the DOM.
- **CSS selectors** (e.g., $('.product-name')) are used to extract the product name, price, and description.

Limitations of Cheerio:

86

- **Cheerio** is ideal for scraping static pages but not for scraping dynamic content loaded by JavaScript. If a webpage uses JavaScript to render content (e.g., via AJAX calls), Cheerio will not be able to extract that content directly.

2. Puppeteer: A Headless Browser for Dynamic Content

If you need to scrape **dynamic content** that is rendered by JavaScript (e.g., content that appears after the page loads or due to user interaction), **Puppeteer** is a better choice. Puppeteer is a Node library that provides a high-level API to control Chrome or Chromium browsers in headless mode (i.e., without a graphical user interface). It allows you to programmatically interact with web pages, including executing JavaScript, capturing screenshots, and scraping dynamic content.

Installing Puppeteer:

To install Puppeteer, run:

```bash
npm install puppeteer
```

Example: Scraping Product Data Using Puppeteer

```javascript

const puppeteer = require('puppeteer');

async function scrapeProductData() {
  // Launch a headless browser instance
  const browser = await puppeteer.launch();
  const page = await browser.newPage();

  // Go to the product page
  await
page.goto('https://example.com/products',      {
waitUntil: 'domcontentloaded' });

  // Scrape product data from the page
  const products = await page.evaluate(() => {
    const productList = [];
    const             productElements      =
document.querySelectorAll('.product');

    productElements.forEach((product) => {
      const           name            =
product.querySelector('.product-
name').innerText;
      const            price           =
product.querySelector('.product-
price').innerText;
```

```
    const          description          =
product.querySelector('.product-
description').innerText;

      productList.push({      name,      price,
description });
    });

    return productList;
  });

  // Log the scraped product data
  console.log(products);

  // Close the browser
  await browser.close();
}

scrapeProductData();
```

Explanation:

- **Puppeteer** launches a headless browser, navigates to the page, and waits for the content to load.
- The **page.evaluate()** method is used to execute code within the context of the page. This allows you to query the DOM for product data, even if it is rendered dynamically by JavaScript.

89

- The script logs the scraped data (product name, price, and description) to the console.

Advantages of Puppeteer:

- **Handles dynamic content**: Puppeteer can scrape content rendered by JavaScript and can even simulate user interactions like scrolling, clicking, and typing.
- **Headless browsing**: Puppeteer runs without opening a visible browser window, making it efficient for scraping.

Limitations of Puppeteer:

- **Performance**: Since Puppeteer uses a full browser instance, it can be slower than Cheerio, especially when scraping multiple pages or when working with large amounts of data.

Real-World Example: Scraping Product Data from E-Commerce Sites

Let's put our knowledge into practice by building a more comprehensive example where we scrape product information from an e-commerce site. We'll use **Puppeteer** to handle dynamic content and **Cheerio** for simpler static content scraping.

Example: Scraping Product Data from an E-Commerce Site (Dynamic Page)

```javascript
const puppeteer = require('puppeteer');

async function scrapeEcommerceData() {
  // Launch a browser
  const browser = await puppeteer.launch();
  const page = await browser.newPage();

  // Visit the e-commerce website
  await page.goto('https://example.com/products',      {
waitUntil: 'load', timeout: 0 });

  // Wait for the product list to load
  await page.waitForSelector('.product-list');

  // Scrape product information
  const products = await page.evaluate(() => {
    const items = [];
    const             productElements             =
document.querySelectorAll('.product');

    productElements.forEach((product) => {
```

```
        const            name            =
product.querySelector('.product-
name').innerText;
        const            price           =
product.querySelector('.product-
price').innerText;
        const            rating          =
product.querySelector('.product-
rating').innerText;

    items.push({ name, price, rating });
  });

  return items;
});

// Display the results
console.log('Scraped Products:', products);

// Close the browser
await browser.close();
}

scrapeEcommerceData();
```

Explanation:

- **waitForSelector()** ensures the page has loaded the necessary elements before attempting to scrape them.

92

- **page.evaluate()** is used to extract data from the rendered HTML content, allowing you to work with dynamic data generated by JavaScript.
- This script scrapes product names, prices, and ratings from an e-commerce site and logs them to the console.

Best Practices and Legal Considerations for Web Scraping

When implementing web scraping, it's important to consider the following:

1. **Respect the Website's robots.txt File**: This file indicates whether a site allows automated scraping. Check the site's robots.txt to see if scraping is allowed, especially for sensitive data.

2. **Avoid Overloading the Server**: Scraping can place a load on the website's server. Implement techniques like rate limiting (e.g., wait between requests) and avoid scraping too frequently.

3. **Check the Terms of Service**: Ensure that scraping does not violate the website's terms of service. Some websites may explicitly prohibit scraping.

4. **Handle Errors Gracefully**: Websites can change their layout or block your IP. Always handle errors (e.g., by checking for broken links or missing elements) and respect the website's resources.

In this chapter, we've covered how to scrape data from websites using **Cheerio** for static content and **Puppeteer** for dynamic content. We explored how to fetch product data from e-commerce websites, a real-world example of automating data collection, and the best practices for ethical web scraping. These techniques will help you automate data collection and analysis tasks in various domains, from e-commerce to news aggregation.

CHAPTER 9

INTRODUCTION TO TASK AUTOMATION LIBRARIES

Overview of Popular Libraries Like Grunt, Gulp, and Webpack

In this chapter, we'll explore some of the most widely used **task automation libraries** in the JavaScript ecosystem: **Grunt**, **Gulp**, and **Webpack**. These tools help developers automate common tasks, such as minification, file compilation, testing, and deployment, making the development process more efficient.

1. Grunt

Grunt is one of the earliest task automation tools in the JavaScript community. It's a JavaScript task runner that allows developers to automate repetitive tasks like minification, linting, testing, and more. Grunt tasks are defined in a configuration file (usually `Gruntfile.js`), and it uses a modular plugin-based system.

95

Key Features:

- **Plugin-Based**: Grunt has a large ecosystem of plugins to handle different tasks, such as image optimization, code linting, and file watching.
- **Configuration-Driven**: Tasks are configured in a `Gruntfile.js`, and you define each task in the configuration.
- **Simple and Lightweight**: Ideal for smaller projects or those looking for a configuration-heavy tool.

Example of a Basic Grunt Setup:

1. **Install Grunt and Grunt CLI**:

bash

```
npm install grunt --save-dev
npm install grunt-cli --save-dev
```

2. **Create Gruntfile.js**:

javascript

```
module.exports = function(grunt) {
  grunt.initConfig({
    pkg: grunt.file.readJSON('package.json'),

    // Minify JavaScript files
```

```
  uglify: {
    build: {
      src: 'src/js/*.js',
      dest: 'dist/js/app.min.js'
    }
  }
});

// Load the plugin
grunt.loadNpmTasks('grunt-contrib-uglify');

// Register the default task
grunt.registerTask('default', ['uglify']);
};
```

Explanation:

- The Gruntfile configures a task (uglify) to minify JavaScript files.
- Running grunt from the command line will execute the default task and minify the specified files.

2. Gulp

Gulp is another task automation tool that aims to be more stream-oriented and faster than Grunt. Gulp uses **streams** to process files, meaning tasks can be chained together in a pipeline for better performance and flexibility.

Key Features:

- **Stream-Based**: Gulp processes files as streams, meaning data is piped through various transformations.
- **Code Over Configuration**: Unlike Grunt, which is configuration-driven, Gulp focuses on code, making it more programmatic and flexible.
- **Faster Execution**: Gulp is often faster than Grunt due to its use of streams and minimal configuration.

Example of a Basic Gulp Setup:

1. **Install Gulp**:

bash

```bash
npm install gulp --save-dev
```

2. **Create gulpfile.js**:

javascript

```javascript
const gulp = require('gulp');
const uglify = require('gulp-uglify');

// Define a task to minify JavaScript
gulp.task('minify-js', () => {
  return gulp.src('src/js/*.js')   // Get all JS
files from the 'src/js' folder
```

98

```
    .pipe(uglify())              // Minify the
JavaScript
    .pipe(gulp.dest('dist/js'));  // Output the
minified file to 'dist/js'
});


// Register the default task
gulp.task('default', gulp.series('minify-js'));
```

Explanation:

- **Gulp** uses streams, so we use `gulp.src()` to load files, `pipe()` to apply transformations, and `gulp.dest()` to output the files.
- The `default` task runs `minify-js`, which processes JavaScript files and minifies them.

3. Webpack

Webpack is a more advanced tool, typically used for bundling JavaScript files and other assets (like images, CSS, etc.). It's widely used in modern front-end development for handling large and complex applications. Webpack allows developers to bundle multiple files into a single output file, manage dependencies, and run loaders to process assets before bundling.

Key Features:

- **Module Bundling**: Webpack bundles JavaScript files and dependencies into a single output file or multiple chunks.
- **Loaders**: Use loaders to transform files before bundling (e.g., compiling Sass to CSS, transpiling ES6 to ES5).
- **Plugins**: Use plugins to perform various tasks like minification, optimization, and environment setup.

Example of a Basic Webpack Setup:

1. **Install Webpack**:

bash

```
npm install webpack webpack-cli --save-dev
```

2. **Create `webpack.config.js`**:

javascript

```
const path = require('path');

module.exports = {
  entry: './src/index.js',   // Entry point for
the application
  output: {
    filename: 'bundle.js',  // Output bundle file
    path: path.resolve(__dirname, 'dist')   //
Output directory
  },
```

```
module: {
  rules: [
    {
      test: /\.js$/,   // Match all JavaScript
files
      exclude: /node_modules/,
      use: 'babel-loader'   // Use Babel to
transpile JavaScript
    }
  ]
},
mode: 'development'   // Set the mode to
development (for easier debugging)
};
```

Explanation:

- **Entry**: Defines the entry point for the application (`./src/index.js`).
- **Output**: Specifies where to output the bundled JavaScript (`dist/bundle.js`).
- **Loaders**: Use the `babel-loader` to transpile ES6+ JavaScript to ES5.
- **Mode**: Set to `development` for unminified output and easier debugging.

How to Integrate JavaScript Automation with These Tools

Task automation tools like Grunt, Gulp, and Webpack integrate well with JavaScript projects, allowing you to automate various tasks such as minification, bundling, testing, and deployment.

Integrating Grunt with a JavaScript Project

To integrate **Grunt** into a project, you can define specific tasks in the Gruntfile and run them from the command line.

- Install the necessary Grunt plugins for the tasks you want to automate (e.g., `grunt-contrib-uglify` for minification).
- Define the tasks in your `Gruntfile.js` and configure them as needed.
- Use the `grunt` command to run the tasks.

Integrating Gulp with a JavaScript Project

To integrate **Gulp**, you can use its programmatic approach to chaining tasks and creating build pipelines:

- Install Gulp and the required plugins for your tasks (e.g., `gulp-uglify` for minifying JS).
- Define tasks in the `gulpfile.js`.
- Run the tasks with `gulp` from the command line.

Integrating Webpack with a JavaScript Project

To integrate **Webpack**:

- Install Webpack and the necessary loaders and plugins.
- Configure the `webpack.config.js` file to define how your assets should be bundled.
- Run Webpack with `npx webpack` or add it as an npm script.

Automating Build and Deployment Processes

One of the most powerful use cases for these task automation libraries is automating the build and deployment process. This ensures that your code is consistently built, tested, and deployed with minimal manual intervention.

Automating Build with Webpack

You can use Webpack to bundle your JavaScript files and assets, ensuring that your application is optimized for production.

1. **Add a Build Script** in your `package.json`:

```json
{
```

103

```
"scripts": {
  "build": "webpack --mode production"
}
}
```

2. **Run the Build**:

```bash
bash
```

```
npm run build
```

This command will bundle your JavaScript and assets for production, applying optimizations like minification.

Automating Deployment with Gulp

You can automate deployment tasks (e.g., uploading files to a server, ing build files to the appropriate directories) with Gulp.

Example of a simple deployment task using **gulp-sftp** to upload files to a remote server:

1. **Install Gulp SFTP**:

```bash
bash
```

```
npm install gulp-sftp --save-dev
```

2. **Define the deployment task** in gulpfile.js:

javascript

```javascript
const gulp = require('gulp');
const sftp = require('gulp-sftp');

gulp.task('deploy', () => {
  return gulp.src('dist/**/*')
    .pipe(sftp({
      host: 'your.server.com',
      user: 'your-username',
      pass: 'your-password',
      remotePath: '/path/to/remote/folder'
    }));
});
```

3. **Run the Deployment Task**:

bash

```bash
gulp deploy
```

This task will upload the build files in the `dist` directory to the remote server.

Conclusion

In this chapter, we've introduced popular **task automation libraries** like **Grunt**, **Gulp**, and **Webpack**, and explored how

105

they can be integrated into JavaScript projects to automate tasks such as minification, bundling, testing, and deployment.

- **Grunt** is great for simple, configuration-driven tasks.
- **Gulp** provides a more flexible, code-driven approach with streams.
- **Webpack** is the go-to tool for bundling JavaScript files and assets in modern front-end development.

These tools not only save time and reduce human error but also streamline the build and deployment processes, making it easier to manage large and complex JavaScript projects.

CHAPTER 10

AUTOMATING BROWSER ACTIONS WITH JAVASCRIPT

Using Puppeteer for Automating Browser Interactions

Puppeteer is a powerful Node.js library used for controlling **headless browsers**, particularly Google Chrome or Chromium. It provides a high-level API that allows developers to automate a wide range of browser tasks, such as navigation, scraping content, interacting with forms, clicking buttons, taking screenshots, and more. Puppeteer is particularly useful for automating tasks on web pages that require interaction or dynamic content loading, such as filling out forms or scraping JavaScript-rendered content.

A **headless browser** is one that runs without a graphical user interface (GUI). Puppeteer's headless mode allows you to automate browser actions without opening a visible browser window, making it more efficient for tasks that don't require human intervention.

Key Features of Puppeteer:

- Automate tasks like clicking, typing, and navigating web pages.
- Scrape dynamic content from JavaScript-heavy websites.
- Take screenshots and generate PDFs.
- Run browser tests or simulate user interactions.
- Perform automation in headless mode, which is faster than running a full browser.

Real-World Example: Automating Login and Form Submissions

One of the most common use cases for Puppeteer is automating interactions with websites that require user input, such as **logging in** and **submitting forms**. We'll walk through an example where we automate the process of logging into a website and submitting a form.

Step 1: Install Puppeteer

To begin, install **Puppeteer** in your project:

```bash
bash
```

```
npm install puppeteer
```

Step 2: Automating Login and Form Submission

In this example, we'll automate logging into a website and submitting a form. For demonstration purposes, let's assume we are automating the login form and submitting a survey.

```javascript
const puppeteer = require('puppeteer');

async function automateLoginAndSubmitForm() {
  // Launch a headless browser
  const browser = await puppeteer.launch({
headless: true }); // Set headless: false to see
the browser
  const page = await browser.newPage();

  // Go to the login page
  await page.goto('https://example.com/login');

  // Fill in the login form and submit
  await page.type('#username', 'yourUsername');
// Replace with the actual selector for the
username field
  await page.type('#password', 'yourPassword');
// Replace with the actual selector for the
password field
  await page.click('#loginButton'); // Replace
with the actual selector for the login button
```

```
  // Wait for the next page to load (e.g.,
dashboard or home page)
  await    page.waitForNavigation({   waitUntil:
'networkidle0' });


  // Now,  let's  automate  filling  out  and
submitting a form
  await page.goto('https://example.com/survey');


  // Fill out the survey form
  await   page.type('#question1',   'Answer   to
question 1');   // Replace  with  the  actual
selectors for the form fields
  await   page.type('#question2',   'Answer   to
question 2');


  // Submit the form
  await page.click('#submitButton');  // Replace
with the actual selector for the submit button


  // Wait for the form submission confirmation
  await    page.waitForSelector('.confirmation-
message');    //   Replace   with   the   actual
confirmation message selector
  console.log('Form submitted successfully!');


  // Close the browser
  await browser.close();
}
```

```
automateLoginAndSubmitForm();
```

Explanation:

- **puppeteer.launch()**: Launches a headless browser.
- **page.goto()**: Navigates to the specified URL.
- **page.type()**: Types the specified text into a form field.
- **page.click()**: Clicks a button or link on the page.
- **page.waitForNavigation()**: Waits for a page to load after a navigation action, such as clicking a button or submitting a form.
- **page.waitForSelector()**: Waits for an element to appear in the DOM (e.g., a confirmation message after submitting the form).

This script automates the login and form submission process, making it a practical tool for tasks like account creation, form-based surveys, or any scenario that involves repetitive form-filling tasks.

Headless Browser Automation

Headless mode refers to running a browser without a graphical user interface. In headless mode, Puppeteer interacts with the browser's DOM just like a regular browser but without opening a window on your screen. This mode is faster and more efficient for

111

automation tasks because it eliminates the overhead of rendering the user interface.

Advantages of Headless Browser Automation:

- **Faster Execution**: Without rendering the user interface, headless mode can execute tasks more quickly.
- **No GUI Overhead**: It's ideal for automated testing, scraping, or batch processing tasks that don't require a visual display.
- **Resource Efficiency**: Headless browsers use fewer system resources (memory and CPU) since they don't need to display the UI.

Running Puppeteer in Headless Mode: By default, Puppeteer runs in **headless mode**. However, if you want to see the browser while it's running, you can set `headless: false` when launching Puppeteer:

```javascript

const browser = await puppeteer.launch({
headless: false }); // This will open a visible browser window
```

To run Puppeteer in **headless mode** (which is the default), simply omit the `headless` option or explicitly set it to `true`:

```
javascript
```

```javascript
const browser = await puppeteer.launch({
headless: true }); // Headless mode is enabled
```

Headless browser automation with Puppeteer is particularly useful for automating tasks such as:

- **Web scraping**: Extracting content from web pages without requiring a GUI.
- **Automated testing**: Running end-to-end tests on websites or applications.
- **Form submissions**: Automating repetitive form-filling tasks (e.g., registration forms, surveys).

Real-World Example: Scraping Data and Navigating Pages with Puppeteer

Let's extend our automation skills by automating a task that involves scraping data from a dynamic webpage. For example, suppose we want to scrape product details from an e-commerce website.

```
javascript
```

```javascript
const puppeteer = require('puppeteer');
```

```
async function scrapeEcommerceData() {
  // Launch a headless browser
  const browser = await puppeteer.launch({
headless: true });
  const page = await browser.newPage();

  // Go to the e-commerce website
  await
page.goto('https://example.com/products');

  // Wait for product list to be available
  await page.waitForSelector('.product-list');

  // Scrape product data
  const products = await page.evaluate(() => {
    const productList = [];
    const items =
document.querySelectorAll('.product-item');
    items.forEach(item => {
      const name = item.querySelector('.product-
name').innerText;
      const price =
item.querySelector('.product-price').innerText;
      productList.push({ name, price });
    });
    return productList;
  });

  console.log('Scraped Products:', products);
```

```
// Close the browser
await browser.close();
}
```

```
scrapeEcommerceData();
```

Explanation:

- **page.evaluate()**: This method allows you to execute JavaScript within the context of the page. We use it to extract product data from the page.
- The script logs a list of products, including their name and price, which can be used for further processing or analysis.

This kind of automation is particularly useful when dealing with **dynamic web pages** where content is loaded by JavaScript.

Handling Dynamic Content and Interaction

Puppeteer is highly effective when dealing with **dynamic content** on websites. For instance, if a page loads content via AJAX or user actions (e.g., clicking a button to reveal more products), you can automate the interaction and wait for the content to load.

Example: Infinite Scroll Automation:

115

Let's automate the process of clicking a "Load More" button on a page with infinite scrolling.

javascript

```
const puppeteer = require('puppeteer');

async function scrapeWithInfiniteScroll() {
  const browser = await puppeteer.launch({
headless: true });
  const page = await browser.newPage();

  await
page.goto('https://example.com/products');

  // Infinite scroll: Scroll until the "Load
More" button is no longer available
  let loadMoreButtonVisible = true;
  while (loadMoreButtonVisible) {
    loadMoreButtonVisible = await page.$('#load-
more-button') !== null;  // Check if the "Load
More" button is visible
    if (loadMoreButtonVisible) {
      await page.click('#load-more-button');
      await page.waitForTimeout(2000);  // Wait
for new products to load
    }
  }
```

```
  // Scrape product data
  const products = await page.evaluate(() => {
    const productList = [];
    const                   items                =
document.querySelectorAll('.product-item');
    items.forEach(item => {
      const name = item.querySelector('.product-
name').innerText;
      const                price                =
item.querySelector('.product-price').innerText;
      productList.push({ name, price });
    });
    return productList;
  });

  console.log('Scraped Products:', products);

  await browser.close();
}

scrapeWithInfiniteScroll();
```

Explanation:

- This script clicks the "Load More" button until it is no longer available, simulating an infinite scroll experience.
- After all the content is loaded, it scrapes the product data.

Conclusion

In this chapter, we explored how to automate browser interactions using **Puppeteer**, including logging into websites, submitting forms, and scraping dynamic content. Puppeteer's ability to control headless browsers allows for powerful and flexible automation tasks, from interacting with web pages to scraping data from complex sites.

Whether you're automating form submissions, scraping product data, or testing web applications, Puppeteer is an excellent choice for any task that involves browser automation. Its headless mode offers an efficient way to execute tasks quickly, and its ability to handle dynamic content makes it indispensable for modern web automation.

CHAPTER 11

AUTOMATING TESTING WITH JAVASCRIPT

Introduction to Test-Driven Development (TDD)

Test-Driven Development (TDD) is a software development practice where tests are written before writing the actual code. It's an iterative process that helps ensure the correctness and functionality of your code by enforcing a strict workflow for testing and development. TDD is used to drive the design of the code and ensures that the code meets the requirements and functions as expected.

The TDD Process typically follows this cycle:

1. **Write a Test**: Start by writing a test that defines a function or improvement you want to add. The test is typically designed to fail at this stage, as the feature hasn't been implemented yet.
2. **Run the Test**: Run the test and see it fail. This step ensures that the test is valid and will fail if the functionality is missing or incorrect.

119

3. **Write the Code**: Write the minimum amount of code necessary to make the test pass.

4. **Refactor**: Once the test passes, refactor the code to improve its quality without changing its functionality.

5. **Repeat**: Add more tests for new functionality, and continue the process iteratively.

By following the TDD approach, developers can improve the quality of their code, ensure that each feature is properly tested, and catch bugs early in the development process.

Using Mocha, Chai, and Jasmine for Automated Testing

In JavaScript, several testing libraries and frameworks are available to facilitate TDD and other types of testing. Some of the most popular tools include **Mocha**, **Chai**, and **Jasmine**. Let's explore each of these tools and how they can be used to automate testing.

1. Mocha

Mocha is a widely used test framework for JavaScript, especially for Node.js applications. It provides a flexible and easy-to-use structure for organizing and running tests. Mocha allows you to run tests in any order, supports multiple assertion libraries, and is highly extensible.

- **Features of Mocha**:
  - Supports asynchronous testing (using callbacks, promises, or async/await).
  - Provides hooks like `before()`, `after()`, `beforeEach()`, and `afterEach()` to run setup and teardown logic.
  - Integrates well with other assertion libraries like Chai and spies like Sinon.

Installing Mocha:

```bash
npm install mocha --save-dev
```

Basic Mocha Test Example:

```javascript
const assert = require('assert');

// Simple function to be tested
function add(a, b) {
  return a + b;
}

// Mocha test case
describe('add()', function() {
```

121

```
it('should return the sum of two numbers',
function() {
    assert.equal(add(2, 3), 5);
  });
});
```

- **describe()**: Organizes tests into groups (suites).
- **it()**: Defines individual test cases.
- **assert.equal()**: Asserts that the expected value equals the actual value.

To run the test, use the following command:

```bash
```

```
npx mocha
```

2. Chai

Chai is an assertion library that can be used with Mocha to provide a variety of ways to check the correctness of your code. It offers several different styles for assertions, including **expect**, **should**, and **assert**.

Installing Chai:

```bash
```

```
npm install chai --save-dev
```

122

Basic Chai Test Example:

```javascript
const chai = require('chai');
const expect = chai.expect;

// Simple function to be tested
function add(a, b) {
  return a + b;
}

// Mocha with Chai assertion
describe('add()', function() {
  it('should return the sum of two numbers',
function() {
    expect(add(2, 3)).to.equal(5);
  });
});
```

- **expect()**: Chai's expect syntax provides a more readable and expressive way to write assertions.
- **.to.equal()**: Checks if the actual value matches the expected value.

3. Jasmine

Jasmine is another popular testing framework, especially for behavior-driven development (BDD). It provides a more

123

opinionated structure for writing tests compared to Mocha. Jasmine comes with built-in assertions and spies for mocking and spying on functions.

Installing Jasmine:

```bash
npm install jasmine --save-dev
```

Basic Jasmine Test Example:

```javascript
const add = (a, b) => a + b;

// Jasmine test case
describe('add()', function() {
  it('should return the sum of two numbers', function() {
    expect(add(2, 3)).toBe(5);
  });
});
```

- **describe()**: Groups the test cases into suites.
- **it()**: Defines an individual test case.
- **expect()**: Used for making assertions.
- **.toBe()**: Checks strict equality, similar to `assert.equal()` in Mocha.

Running Jasmine Tests:

```bash
npx jasmine
```

Automating Unit Tests and Integration Tests

Automated testing involves both **unit tests** and **integration tests**.

- **Unit Tests**: Test individual units of functionality, such as functions or methods. Unit tests are typically isolated and mock dependencies to focus on the unit being tested.

  Example: Testing a simple function:

```javascript
function multiply(a, b) {
  return a * b;
}

describe('multiply()', function() {
  it('should return the product of two
numbers', function() {
    expect(multiply(2, 3)).toBe(6);
  });
});
```

125

- **Integration Tests**: Test how different parts of the application work together. These tests often involve interacting with external systems like databases or APIs and ensure that components integrate as expected.

Example: Testing an API endpoint (using Mocha, Chai, and supertest):

bash

```
npm install supertest --save-dev
javascript
```

```javascript
const request = require('supertest');
const app = require('../app');   // Your Express app or server

describe('GET /users', function() {
  it('should return a list of users', function(done) {
    request(app)
      .get('/users')
      .expect(200)
      .end(function(err, res) {
        if (err) return done(err);

expect(res.body).to.be.an('array');
        done();
      });
```

126

```
    });
});
```

- supertest is a library used to test HTTP APIs by simulating requests and checking the responses.

Best Practices for Automated Testing

To make the most out of automated testing with JavaScript, consider the following best practices:

1. **Write Tests First**: Follow **Test-Driven Development (TDD)** where you write tests before implementing the functionality. This ensures that your code meets the required behavior and avoids unnecessary complexity.
2. **Keep Tests Isolated**: Ensure that each unit test is independent and does not rely on external systems (like a database). Use mocks or stubs to isolate dependencies.
3. **Automate Regression Tests**: As your application grows, automate regression tests to catch bugs introduced by new code. This ensures that previously working features continue to function as expected.
4. **Run Tests Frequently**: Use continuous integration (CI) tools like **Jenkins, Travis CI**, or **GitHub Actions** to run

tests automatically whenever you push new changes to your codebase. This helps catch errors early.

5. **Test Both Happy and Edge Cases**: Write tests for both common scenarios (happy path) and edge cases (e.g., invalid input, empty values, and error conditions).

Conclusion

In this chapter, we've explored **automated testing** using JavaScript and introduced the key concepts behind **Test-Driven Development (TDD)**. We also covered the use of popular testing libraries like **Mocha**, **Chai**, and **Jasmine** for both unit and integration testing.

By automating your tests, you can ensure the stability and correctness of your code, reduce the likelihood of bugs, and improve overall software quality. With the tools and practices described in this chapter, you'll be able to automate your testing process and integrate it seamlessly into your development workflow, allowing for more reliable and maintainable software.

CHAPTER 12

CONTINUOUS INTEGRATION AND DEPLOYMENT (CI/CD) WITH JAVASCRIPT

Setting Up CI/CD Pipelines with JavaScript

Continuous Integration (CI) and **Continuous Deployment (CD)** are essential practices in modern software development. CI focuses on automatically integrating code changes into the shared codebase, while CD automates the deployment of code to production environments.

CI/CD pipelines automate the entire process—from building and testing code to deploying it to various environments—ensuring that code is always in a deployable state and can be released quickly and reliably.

Key Concepts of CI/CD:

- **Continuous Integration (CI)**: Developers merge their changes into a central repository frequently (usually multiple times per day). Every change triggers automated builds and tests to ensure the new code doesn't break the application.

- **Continuous Deployment (CD)**: After the code passes the tests in CI, it is automatically deployed to production or staging environments without manual intervention.
- **Continuous Delivery (CD)**: Similar to Continuous Deployment, but here the deployment step requires manual approval before the code is released to production.

The Benefits of CI/CD:

- **Faster development cycles**: Automates testing and deployment, allowing faster and more frequent releases.
- **Improved quality**: Continuous testing ensures that defects are detected early, reducing bugs in production.
- **Efficient feedback**: Automated feedback from CI/CD pipelines helps developers identify and fix issues quickly.

Automating the Deployment Process with Node.js

To automate the deployment of a Node.js application, the CI/CD pipeline needs to handle tasks such as:

1. **Installing dependencies**.
2. **Running tests** to ensure the code is functional and doesn't introduce new bugs.
3. **Building** the application (if necessary).

4. **Deploying** the application to a staging or production server.

Node.js-based applications are often deployed to cloud platforms like **Heroku**, **AWS**, or **DigitalOcean**, and CI/CD pipelines can be set up to automate this process.

Example: Automating Deployment to Heroku with Node.js

Heroku provides an easy-to-use platform for deploying Node.js applications. You can automate deployment to Heroku by integrating your CI/CD pipeline with services like GitHub Actions or Travis CI.

Here's how to automate deployment to **Heroku** with a Node.js app:

1. **Install Heroku CLI**: First, you need to install the Heroku CLI on your local machine or CI/CD runner.
2. **Set up Heroku API Key**: For CI/CD tools to authenticate and deploy, you need to set up an API key from Heroku. You can find this in the **Account Settings** on the Heroku Dashboard.

   Run the following command to generate an API key:

   ```bash
   bash
   ```

   ```
   heroku auth:token
   ```

3. **Set Up Deployment Script**: Create a **deployment script** that pushes the code to Heroku. You can use the `git` command to deploy the code to Heroku.

    Example `deploy.sh` script:

    ```bash
    bash

    #!/bin/bash
    echo "Deploying to Heroku..."

    # Set Heroku app name (replace 'your-app-name' with the actual app name)
    HEROKU_APP_NAME="your-app-name"

    # Login to Heroku
    echo $HEROKU_API_KEY | heroku auth:token

    # Push the code to Heroku
    git                        push
    https://git.heroku.com/$HEROKU_APP_NAME.g
    it master
    ```

Real-World Example: Deploying a Web App with GitHub Actions

GitHub Actions provides an easy way to automate workflows directly in GitHub. You can set up CI/CD pipelines within your

GitHub repository to build, test, and deploy your Node.js web application.

Example: Setting Up a CI/CD Pipeline with GitHub Actions for a Node.js App

1. **Create the GitHub Workflow File**: GitHub Actions workflows are stored in the `.github/workflows/` directory of your repository. Create a YAML file for your workflow. For instance, name it `ci-cd-pipeline.yml`.

2. **Define the Workflow in YAML**: The YAML file defines the CI/CD pipeline steps, including installing dependencies, running tests, and deploying the app.

Example `ci-cd-pipeline.yml` for Node.js app:

```yaml
yaml

name: Node.js CI/CD Pipeline

on:
  push:
    branches:
      - main  # Trigger pipeline on push to main branch
  pull_request:
    branches:
      - main  # Trigger pipeline on pull request to main branch
```

133

```
jobs:
  build:
    runs-on: ubuntu-latest

    steps:
      # Step 1: Checkout code from GitHub
repository
      - name: Checkout repository
        uses: actions/checkout@v2

      # Step 2: Set up Node.js environment
      - name: Set up Node.js
        uses: actions/setup-node@v2
        with:
          node-version: '14'  # Specify the
Node.js version

      # Step 3: Install dependencies
      - name: Install dependencies
        run: npm install

      # Step 4: Run tests
      - name: Run tests
        run: npm test

      # Step 5: Deploy to Heroku
      - name: Deploy to Heroku
```

```
        uses:  akshatmittal/heroku-deploy-
action@v1
        with:
          heroku_email:              ${{
secrets.HEROKU_EMAIL }}
          heroku_api_key:            ${{
secrets.HEROKU_API_KEY }}
          heroku_app_name:   'your-heroku-
app-name'
          heroku_branch: 'main'
```

Explanation:

- **on.push**: The workflow triggers every time you push changes to the `main` branch of the repository.

- **Steps**:
  - **Checkout code**: The `actions/checkout` action checks out the code from your repository.
  - **Set up Node.js**: The `actions/setup-node` action installs the required version of Node.js.
  - **Install dependencies**: The `npm install` command installs all dependencies listed in your `package.json`.

- **Run tests**: The `npm test` command runs your tests to ensure the code is working as expected.
- **Deploy to Heroku**: The deployment step uses the `heroku-deploy-action` to push your app to Heroku.

3. **Add Heroku Credentials to GitHub Secrets**: To securely authenticate with Heroku, add your Heroku email and API key as **GitHub Secrets**:

   o **HEROKU_EMAIL**: Your Heroku account email.

   o **HEROKU_API_KEY**: Your Heroku API key, generated earlier.

   To add secrets:

   o Go to your GitHub repository's **Settings** → **Secrets**.

   o Click on **New repository secret** and add `HEROKU_EMAIL` and `HEROKU_API_KEY`.

4. **Run the Workflow**: Once you commit and push your changes to the `main` branch, GitHub Actions will automatically run the workflow. It will:

   o Install dependencies.

   o Run tests.

   o Deploy your Node.js app to Heroku.

136

Benefits of Using CI/CD for Node.js Applications

1. **Automated Testing**: Every time you push new code to your repository, your CI pipeline will automatically run tests. This ensures that new changes do not introduce bugs or regressions into your application.

2. **Faster Deployment**: By automating the deployment process, you reduce the time required to deploy updates to production. This allows you to release features and bug fixes faster.

3. **Improved Code Quality**: With automated testing and deployment, you are more likely to catch issues early in the development process, improving the overall quality of the code.

4. **Seamless Collaboration**: With CI/CD, team members can easily contribute to the project without worrying about conflicts or manual deployment steps. Code is continuously integrated and deployed, ensuring that everyone works with the most up-to-date version.

Conclusion

In this chapter, we've explored how to set up **Continuous Integration (CI)** and **Continuous Deployment (CD)** pipelines for Node.js applications. We covered how to automate the process of building, testing, and deploying your web apps using tools like **GitHub Actions**.

By automating these processes, you can achieve faster, more reliable releases, minimize human error, and improve overall productivity. Whether you're working on small projects or large-scale applications, implementing CI/CD pipelines will streamline your development workflow and ensure that your code is always ready for production.

CHAPTER 13

AUTOMATING DATA ANALYSIS AND VISUALIZATION WITH JAVASCRIPT

Using JavaScript for Data Manipulation and Analysis

JavaScript is not only a powerful tool for web development but also for **data manipulation** and **analysis**. With the rise of data-driven decision-making in various industries, it's crucial to understand how JavaScript can be used to process, analyze, and visualize data.

JavaScript offers several built-in methods and third-party libraries to help manipulate data efficiently, making it a strong contender for automating data analysis tasks. Whether it's working with arrays, objects, or external data sources (like APIs or databases), JavaScript has the tools needed for thorough data analysis.

Key JavaScript Concepts for Data Analysis:

- **Arrays and Objects**: Use arrays to hold data sets and objects for storing key-value pairs. You can manipulate

139

data using methods like `.map()`, `.filter()`, `.reduce()`, and `.forEach()`.

- **Higher-order Functions**: JavaScript's first-class functions and array methods make it easy to iterate, aggregate, and transform data.
- **Working with Dates**: JavaScript's `Date` object helps in handling time-based data, which is often crucial in reporting and data analysis tasks.

Example of Data Manipulation: Let's manipulate an array of sales data to calculate the total sales and average sales.

```javascript
const salesData = [
  { product: 'Widget A', sales: 500 },
  { product: 'Widget B', sales: 300 },
  { product: 'Widget C', sales: 450 },
];

// Calculate total sales
const totalSales = salesData.reduce((total, item) => total + item.sales, 0);

// Calculate average sales
const averageSales = totalSales / salesData.length;

console.log('Total Sales:', totalSales);
```

```
console.log('Average Sales:', averageSales);
```

Explanation:

- We use `reduce()` to sum up the sales of all products, which gives us the total sales.
- The average sales are calculated by dividing the total sales by the number of items in the `salesData` array.

JavaScript's array manipulation methods make it simple to transform and analyze data in real-time, automating the process of calculating totals, averages, and more complex metrics.

Automating Data Reporting Tasks with Libraries like D3.js and Chart.js

Once data has been processed and analyzed, the next step is to **visualize** it. Data visualization is crucial for making data comprehensible and actionable. JavaScript has some excellent libraries that can help automate the creation of dynamic, interactive visualizations.

1. D3.js: A Powerful Data Visualization Library

D3.js (Data-Driven Documents) is one of the most powerful and flexible libraries for creating data-driven visualizations. D3 allows you to bind data to a Document Object Model (DOM) and apply data-driven transformations to the document. It provides fine control over the presentation and interaction of data visualizations, allowing you to create interactive and complex visualizations.

- **Features**:
  - Works with any data format (CSV, JSON, XML, etc.).
  - Allows the creation of interactive visualizations (e.g., graphs, maps, and charts).
  - Provides great flexibility in how data is presented.

Example: Creating a Bar Chart with D3.js

html

```html
<!DOCTYPE html>
<html lang="en">
<head>
  <meta charset="UTF-8">
  <meta name="viewport" content="width=device-width, initial-scale=1.0">
  <title>D3 Bar Chart</title>
  <script src="https://d3js.org/d3.v6.min.js"></script>
</head>
<body>
  <svg width="500" height="300"></svg>
```

```
<script>
  const data = [100, 200, 300, 400, 500];

  const svg = d3.select('svg');

  svg.selectAll('rect')
    .data(data)
    .enter()
    .append('rect')
    .attr('x', (d, i) => i * 100)   // Position each bar
    .attr('y', (d) => 300 - d)      // Set height based on data value
    .attr('width', 50)              // Set width of each bar
    .attr('height', (d) => d)       // Set height of each bar
    .attr('fill', 'blue');
  </script>
</body>
</html>
```

Explanation:

- **d3.select('svg')**: Selects the SVG element where the chart will be drawn.
- **selectAll('rect')**: Creates a set of <rect> elements for each data point in the data array.

143

- **enter()**: Ensures that each data point corresponds to a new <rect> element.
- **attr()**: Sets attributes like position, width, height, and color.

This simple bar chart visualizes a dataset as blue bars, with each bar's height corresponding to the data value.

2. Chart.js: A Simple and Easy-to-Use Visualization Library

Chart.js is another popular JavaScript library used to create simple, interactive charts. While it's less flexible than D3.js, it's easier to use and provides a variety of chart types (line, bar, radar, pie, etc.) out of the box.

- **Features**:
  - Simple API for creating various types of charts (line, bar, pie, etc.).
  - Great for dashboards and real-time data visualizations.
  - Interactive charts with tooltips and hover effects.

Example: Creating a Line Chart with Chart.js

html

```
<!DOCTYPE html>
<html lang="en">
```

```
<head>
  <meta charset="UTF-8">
  <meta name="viewport" content="width=device-
width, initial-scale=1.0">
  <title>Chart.js Line Chart</title>
  <script
src="https://cdn.jsdelivr.net/npm/chart.js"></s
cript>
</head>
<body>
  <canvas       id="myChart"       width="400"
height="200"></canvas>
  <script>
    var            ctx              =
document.getElementById('myChart').getContext('
2d');

    var myChart = new Chart(ctx, {
      type: 'line', // Type of chart (line, bar,
etc.)
      data: {
        labels: ['January', 'February', 'March',
'April', 'May'], // X-axis labels
        datasets: [{
          label: 'Sales over time',
          data: [100, 200, 300, 400, 500], // Y-
axis data
          borderColor: 'rgb(75, 192, 192)', //
Line color
```

```
        fill: false, // Disable fill below the
line
      }]
    },
    options: {
      scales: {
        y: {
          beginAtZero: true
        }
      }
    }
  });
  </script>
</body>
</html>
```

Explanation:

- **type: 'line'**: Specifies the type of chart to create (in this case, a line chart).
- **data.labels**: Provides the labels for the X-axis (e.g., months).
- **datasets**: Defines the data to be visualized, with the data array holding the Y-axis values (sales over time).
- **borderColor**: Sets the color of the chart line.
- **fill: false**: Ensures the area under the line is not filled.

Chart.js makes it easy to create a wide variety of charts with minimal setup.

Real-World Example: Generating Sales Reports

Let's put everything together by automating the generation of a **sales report**. In this example, we'll analyze sales data, create a line chart to visualize the sales over time, and display the total sales and average sales.

Step 1: Organize and Analyze Sales Data

```javascript

const salesData = [
   { month: 'January', sales: 500 },
   { month: 'February', sales: 700 },
   { month: 'March', sales: 800 },
   { month: 'April', sales: 600 },
   { month: 'May', sales: 750 },
];

// Calculate total sales and average sales
const totalSales = salesData.reduce((total,
item) => total + item.sales, 0);
const averageSales = totalSales /
salesData.length;
```

```
console.log('Total Sales:', totalSales);
console.log('Average Sales:', averageSales);
```

Step 2: Generate a Line Chart with Chart.js

```html
html

<!DOCTYPE html>
<html lang="en">
<head>
  <meta charset="UTF-8">
  <meta name="viewport" content="width=device-width, initial-scale=1.0">
  <title>Sales Report</title>
  <script src="https://cdn.jsdelivr.net/npm/chart.js"></script>
</head>
<body>
  <h2>Sales Report</h2>
  <canvas id="salesChart" width="400" height="200"></canvas>
  <script>
    const salesData = [500, 700, 800, 600, 750]; // Sales data for the chart
    const months = ['January', 'February', 'March', 'April', 'May']; // Labels
```

148

```javascript
    var              ctx              =
document.getElementById('salesChart').getContex
t('2d');
    var salesChart = new Chart(ctx, {
      type: 'line',
      data: {
        labels: months,
        datasets: [{
          label: 'Monthly Sales',
          data: salesData,
          borderColor: 'rgb(75, 192, 192)',
          fill: false
        }]
      },
      options: {
        scales: {
          y: {
            beginAtZero: true
          }
        }
      }
    });
  </script>
</body>
</html>
```

Step 3: Output the Report

```javascript
javascript
```

```
console.log('Sales Report:');
console.log('Total Sales:', totalSales);
console.log('Average Sales:', averageSales);
```

Conclusion

In this chapter, we explored how JavaScript can be used to automate **data manipulation**, **analysis**, and **visualization**. We demonstrated how to:

- Manipulate and analyze data using built-in JavaScript methods like `reduce()`.
- Use libraries like **D3.js** and **Chart.js** to automate the generation of interactive visualizations such as bar charts and line charts.
- Automate the process of generating and displaying sales reports with JavaScript.

With the power of JavaScript and its visualization libraries, you can automate data reporting tasks and turn raw data into actionable insights in real-time. Whether you're building dashboards, financial reports, or data-driven web applications, these tools enable you to automate and streamline your data analysis workflows.

CHAPTER 14

WORKING WITH DATABASES AND AUTOMATING CRUD OPERATIONS

Introduction to MongoDB and SQL

In web development, **databases** are essential for storing, retrieving, and manipulating data. Two of the most commonly used types of databases are **MongoDB** (a NoSQL database) and **SQL** (Structured Query Language) databases, such as **MySQL** and **PostgreSQL**. Both of these database types allow you to store data, but they are optimized for different use cases.

1. MongoDB (NoSQL Database)

MongoDB is a **NoSQL** database that stores data in **documents** (using a format called BSON, which is similar to JSON). MongoDB is schema-less, which means it doesn't require predefined structures for data, making it very flexible.

- **Advantages**:
  - Schema flexibility (can store different types of data in the same collection).

151

- o Scalable (designed for distributed systems).
- o High performance for read/write operations.
- **Use Cases**:
  - o Applications requiring flexible, unstructured data storage (e.g., blogs, content management systems, e-commerce platforms).

2. SQL Databases (Relational Databases)

SQL databases are **relational databases** that store data in tables with fixed schemas. They use **SQL** queries to interact with the data, which is organized into rows and columns.

- **Advantages**:
  - o Strong data integrity and relationships between tables (using joins, foreign keys).
  - o Well-defined schemas.
  - o Mature ecosystem with tools for querying and administration.
- **Use Cases**:
  - o Applications requiring structured data with relationships (e.g., customer management systems, financial apps, and transactional systems).

Popular SQL Databases:

- **MySQL**: A widely used open-source SQL database.

- **PostgreSQL**: A powerful, open-source relational database that supports advanced queries and data types.

Automating Database Operations with JavaScript

JavaScript, with the help of **Node.js** and various database libraries, makes it easy to automate **CRUD operations** (Create, Read, Update, Delete) for both MongoDB and SQL databases.

1. Working with MongoDB in Node.js

To interact with MongoDB in a Node.js application, we typically use the **MongoDB Node.js Driver** or the more popular **Mongoose** library, which provides a higher-level abstraction.

Installing Mongoose:

```bash
npm install mongoose
```

Example: Automating CRUD Operations in MongoDB

```javascript
const mongoose = require('mongoose');

// Connect to MongoDB
```

153

```
mongoose.connect('mongodb://localhost:27017/myd
b', { useNewUrlParser: true, useUnifiedTopology:
true });

// Define a schema
const userSchema = new mongoose.Schema({
  name: String,
  age: Number,
  email: String
});

// Create a model from the schema
const User = mongoose.model('User', userSchema);

// Automating CRUD operations

// CREATE: Add a new user
async function createUser() {
  const user = new User({
    name: 'John Doe',
    age: 30,
    email: 'john.doe@example.com'
  });
  await user.save();
  console.log('User Created:', user);
}

// READ: Find all users
async function getUsers() {
```

```javascript
  const users = await User.find();
  console.log('Users:', users);
}

// UPDATE: Update a user's details
async function updateUser(userId) {
  const          user          =          await
User.findByIdAndUpdate(userId, { age: 31 }, {
new: true });
  console.log('User Updated:', user);
}

// DELETE: Remove a user
async function deleteUser(userId) {
  const          result          =          await
User.findByIdAndDelete(userId);
  console.log('User Deleted:', result);
}

// Example usage
async function run() {
  await createUser();  // Create a user
  const users = await getUsers();  // Retrieve
users
  await updateUser(users[0]._id); // Update user
  await deleteUser(users[0]._id); // Delete user
}

run();
```

Explanation:

- `mongoose.connect()`: Connects to the MongoDB database.
- **CRUD functions**: Each of the functions (`createUser`, `getUsers`, `updateUser`, `deleteUser`) corresponds to a specific CRUD operation, such as adding, retrieving, updating, and deleting documents in the database.

2. Working with SQL Databases in Node.js

To interact with SQL databases in Node.js, you can use libraries like **mysql2** for MySQL or **pg** for PostgreSQL.

Installing mysql2:

```bash
npm install mysql2
```

Example: Automating CRUD Operations in MySQL

```javascript
const mysql = require('mysql2');

// Create a connection to the MySQL database
const connection = mysql.createConnection({
  host: 'localhost',
```

```javascript
  user: 'root',
  password: 'password',
  database: 'mydb'
});

// Automating CRUD operations

// CREATE: Add a new user
function createUser() {
  connection.query(
    'INSERT INTO users (name, age, email) VALUES
(?, ?, ?)',
    ['John Doe', 30, 'john.doe@example.com'],
    (err, results) => {
      if (err) {
        console.error('Error  creating  user:',
err);
        return;
      }
      console.log('User Created:', results);
    }
  );
}

// READ: Find all users
function getUsers() {
  connection.query('SELECT * FROM users', (err,
results) => {
    if (err) {
```

```
      console.error('Error   fetching   users:',
err);
      return;
    }
    console.log('Users:', results);
  });
}


// UPDATE: Update a user's details
function updateUser(userId) {
  connection.query(
    'UPDATE users SET age = ? WHERE id = ?',
    [31, userId],
    (err, results) => {
      if (err) {
        console.error('Error   updating   user:',
err);
        return;
      }
      console.log('User Updated:', results);
    }
  );
}


// DELETE: Remove a user
function deleteUser(userId) {
  connection.query('DELETE FROM users WHERE id =
?', [userId], (err, results) => {
    if (err) {
```

```
      console.error('Error    deleting    user:',
err);
      return;
    }
    console.log('User Deleted:', results);
  });
}


// Example usage
function run() {
  createUser();  // Create a user
  getUsers();  // Retrieve users
  // You can call updateUser() and deleteUser()
as needed after fetching users
}


run();
```

Explanation:

- **`mysql.createConnection()`**: Establishes a connection to a MySQL database.
- **CRUD functions**: Similar to the MongoDB example, the CRUD operations (create, read, update, delete) are implemented using SQL queries, with each operation interacting with the database.

Real-World Example: Building a Data Backup System

A common requirement for database-driven applications is creating **data backups** to ensure data integrity and prevent data loss. In this example, we will automate the process of creating database backups.

1. Automating MongoDB Backup

To back up a MongoDB database, you can use the `mongodump` utility. You can automate this using JavaScript by invoking system commands using Node.js's **child_process** module.

Example: MongoDB Backup Automation

javascript

```javascript
const { exec } = require('child_process');

// MongoDB backup function
function backupMongoDB() {
  const command = 'mongodump --
uri="mongodb://localhost:27017/mydb" --
out="./backups"';

  exec(command, (err, stdout, stderr) => {
    if (err) {
      console.error('Error creating MongoDB
backup:', err);
```

160

```
    return;
  }
  console.log('Backup created successfully:',
stdout);
  });
}


backupMongoDB();
```

Explanation:

- **exec()**: Executes a system command (mongodump in this case) to back up the MongoDB database to the ./backups directory.

2. Automating SQL Database Backup

For SQL databases, you can use the mysqldump utility to create a backup of a MySQL database. This can also be automated in Node.js using **child_process**.

Example: MySQL Backup Automation

```javascript

const { exec } = require('child_process');

// MySQL backup function
function backupMySQL() {
```

```
  const command = 'mysqldump -u root -p password
mydb > backups/mydb_backup.sql';

  exec(command, (err, stdout, stderr) => {
    if (err) {
      console.error('Error     creating     MySQL
backup:', err);
      return;
    }
    console.log('Backup created successfully:',
stdout);
  });
}

backupMySQL();
```

Explanation:

- **mysqldump**: This command creates a backup of the
  MySQL database `mydb` and saves it to the file
  `mydb_backup.sql` in the `backups` directory.
- The password is provided in the command for
  authentication.

Conclusion

In this chapter, we explored how to **automate database operations** with JavaScript using **MongoDB** and **SQL** databases. We covered:

- Basic CRUD operations in MongoDB using Mongoose and in MySQL using the mysql2 library.
- Real-world examples such as **building a data backup system** for MongoDB and MySQL databases.
- How to leverage JavaScript's capabilities to automate tasks like creating backups, reducing manual intervention, and improving reliability.

By automating these database tasks, you ensure that your applications are more efficient and maintainable, and you prevent the risk of human error in daily operations. Whether you're working with NoSQL or SQL databases, JavaScript provides powerful tools to automate data management and processing tasks.

Y

CHAPTER 15

AUTOMATING EMAIL AND NOTIFICATIONS

Using NodeMailer to Automate Email Sending

One of the most common automation tasks in web development is sending emails. **NodeMailer** is a powerful, easy-to-use Node.js library that allows you to send emails from your Node.js applications. It supports multiple transport methods (like SMTP, sendmail, and SES) and is highly customizable for a variety of use cases, such as sending welcome emails, notifications, or reminders.

1. Installing NodeMailer

To start using **NodeMailer**, you need to install it in your Node.js project.

bash

```
npm install nodemailer
```

2. Basic Setup for Sending Emails

To send an email using NodeMailer, you need to configure an email transport service. The transport configuration contains the details of your email service provider (e.g., Gmail, Outlook, or a custom SMTP server).

Here's a basic example of how to send an email using **Gmail's SMTP server**:

```javascript
const nodemailer = require('nodemailer');

// Create a transporter using Gmail's SMTP server
const transporter = nodemailer.createTransport({
  service: 'gmail',
  auth: {
    user: 'your-email@gmail.com',   // Your Gmail address
    pass: 'your-email-password'     // Your Gmail password or app-specific password
  }
});

// Set up the email options
const mailOptions = {
  from: 'your-email@gmail.com',
  to: 'recipient-email@example.com',
```

165

```
  subject: 'Test Email from NodeMailer',
  text: 'Hello, this is a test email sent using
NodeMailer!'
};


// Send the email
transporter.sendMail(mailOptions, (error, info)
=> {
  if (error) {
    return console.log('Error:', error);
  }
  console.log('Email sent:', info.response);
});
```

Explanation:

- **transporter**: This is the transport configuration for sending the email. It includes the email service provider (Gmail in this case) and your credentials.
- **mailOptions**: Specifies the email details, including sender, recipient, subject, and body content.
- **sendMail()**: This method sends the email and logs the result or any error that occurs during the process.

Note: For Gmail, you might need to generate an **App Password** (if you use 2-step verification) or enable **less secure apps** (not recommended for production). Always use environment variables or configuration files to store sensitive information like passwords.

Setting Up Automated Email Notifications

Automated email notifications are commonly used for sending alerts or reminders, such as:

- Account activity notifications (e.g., login, password change).
- System status alerts (e.g., server downtime).
- Regular reminders (e.g., upcoming events, deadlines).

NodeMailer can be used to automatically send these notifications when triggered by events in your application.

1. Example: Sending Automated Notification on User Registration

Let's say you want to send an automated email notification to a user when they register on your application. This can be done after saving the user's information to your database.

Example: Automated Welcome Email After User Registration

javascript

```
const nodemailer = require('nodemailer');
```

```
// Function to send the welcome email
async function sendWelcomeEmail(userEmail) {
  // Create transporter object
  const                   transporter              =
nodemailer.createTransport({
    service: 'gmail',
    auth: {
      user: 'your-email@gmail.com',
      pass: 'your-email-password'
    }
  });

  // Email options
  const mailOptions = {
    from: 'your-email@gmail.com',
    to: userEmail,
    subject: 'Welcome to Our Service!',
    text: 'Hello! Thank you for registering with
us. We are excited to have you on board.'
  };

  // Send email
  transporter.sendMail(mailOptions,        (error,
info) => {
    if (error) {
      return console.log('Error:', error);
    }
    console.log('Welcome      email      sent:',
info.response);
```

```
  });
}
```

```
// Simulate user registration
const newUserEmail = 'newuser@example.com';
sendWelcomeEmail(newUserEmail);
```

Explanation:

- This function automatically sends a **welcome email** to a user after their registration process is completed (simulated here by passing `newUserEmail`).
- It sets up the email options and sends the email using the `transporter.sendMail()` method.

2. Scheduling Automated Email Notifications

You can also schedule email notifications to be sent at a later time. This is especially useful for sending reminders, alerts, or reports.

For scheduling, you can use the `node-cron` library, which allows you to run scheduled tasks (like sending emails) at fixed intervals.

Install `node-cron`:

```bash
npm install node-cron
```

Example: Send a Daily Reminder Email at 9 AM

javascript

```
const nodemailer = require('nodemailer');
const cron = require('node-cron');

// Function to send reminder email
function sendReminderEmail() {
  const                transporter              =
nodemailer.createTransport({
    service: 'gmail',
    auth: {
      user: 'your-email@gmail.com',
      pass: 'your-email-password'
    }
  });

  const mailOptions = {
    from: 'your-email@gmail.com',
    to: 'recipient@example.com',
    subject: 'Daily Reminder',
    text: 'This  is  your  daily  reminder  to
complete your tasks.'
  };

  transporter.sendMail(mailOptions,        (error,
info) => {
    if (error) {
      return console.log('Error:', error);
```

```
    }
    console.log('Reminder      email      sent:',
info.response);
  });
}


// Schedule a task to send the email every day at
9 AM
cron.schedule('0 9 * * *', sendReminderEmail);
// Cron expression: '0 9 * * *' = 9 AM every day
```

Explanation:

- **node-cron** is used to schedule the `sendReminderEmail` function to run every day at 9 AM.

- The cron expression `'0 9 * * *'` specifies that the task should run at 9:00 AM every day.

Real-World Example: Automating Email Reminders

A **common use case** for email automation is sending reminders for appointments, deadlines, or tasks. We'll create a simple system that sends a **reminder email** 24 hours before a user's appointment.

Steps:

1. **Store Appointment Data**: You'll need to store the user's appointment details (e.g., date and time) in your database.
2. **Calculate Time Difference**: Based on the current time, calculate if an appointment is 24 hours away.
3. **Send Reminder**: If the appointment is within 24 hours, send an automated email reminder.

Example: Appointment Reminder System

javascript

```
const nodemailer = require('nodemailer');
const cron = require('node-cron');

// Example appointment data (this would usually
come from a database)
const appointments = [
  { email: 'user1@example.com', appointmentTime:
'2023-07-20T10:00:00' },
  { email: 'user2@example.com', appointmentTime:
'2023-07-21T14:00:00' }
];

// Function to send reminder email
function sendReminderEmail(appointment) {
  const            transporter            =
nodemailer.createTransport({
```

```
  service: 'gmail',
  auth: {
    user: 'your-email@gmail.com',
    pass: 'your-email-password'
  }
});


const mailOptions = {
  from: 'your-email@gmail.com',
  to: appointment.email,
  subject: 'Appointment Reminder',
  text: `This is a reminder that your
appointment is scheduled for
${appointment.appointmentTime}.`
  };


transporter.sendMail(mailOptions,     (error,
info) => {
    if (error) {
      return console.log('Error:', error);
    }
    console.log('Reminder       sent       to',
appointment.email);
  });
}


// Function to check appointments and send
reminders
function checkAndSendReminders() {
```

```javascript
  const currentTime = new Date();

  appointments.forEach(appointment => {
    const appointmentTime = new Date(appointment.appointmentTime);
    const timeDiff = appointmentTime - currentTime;

    // If appointment is 24 hours away, send reminder
    if (timeDiff <= 86400000 && timeDiff > 0) { // 86400000 ms = 24 hours
      sendReminderEmail(appointment);
    }
  });
}

// Schedule the reminder check every day at 9 AM
cron.schedule('0 9 * * *', checkAndSendReminders);
```

Explanation:

- The **appointments** array holds user appointment data, including the date and time.
- The **checkAndSendReminders()** function checks if any appointment is 24 hours away from the current time. If so, it sends a reminder email using sendReminderEmail().

174

- The **cron job** is set to run daily at 9 AM, ensuring that reminders are checked and sent out daily.

Conclusion

In this chapter, we explored how to **automate email sending** and **notifications** using **NodeMailer** in Node.js. We covered:

- The basics of sending emails with NodeMailer.
- Setting up automated email notifications and scheduling tasks.
- Real-world examples such as sending **welcome emails**, **reminders**, and **appointment notifications**.

By automating email notifications and reminders, you can improve user engagement and keep your users informed, all while saving time and reducing manual effort. The ability to schedule emails, trigger them based on certain conditions, and send notifications automatically makes NodeMailer a valuable tool for any application that requires email communication.

CHAPTER 16

AUTOMATING DATA SYNCHRONIZATION ACROSS PLATFORMS

Synchronizing Data Between Different Services (e.g., Google Sheets to a Database)

In modern applications, data often needs to be synchronized between different platforms and services. For example, you might want to sync data from **Google Sheets** to a **database** or transfer data between a **CRM system** and an **email marketing platform**. By automating this data exchange, you can ensure consistency across your systems and reduce the chances of errors caused by manual updates.

Common Use Cases for Data Synchronization:

- **Syncing data between Google Sheets and a database**: A Google Sheet may serve as an interface for users to input data, and you may want to automatically sync that data to a central database.

- **Syncing CRM data with other tools**: Automatically sync customer relationship management (CRM) data with email marketing platforms, helpdesk systems, or contact management tools like **Google Contacts**.
- **Integrating with third-party APIs**: Many applications expose their data via APIs, and you can use these APIs to synchronize data between platforms.

1. Synchronizing Data from Google Sheets to a Database

Google Sheets is a widely used tool for tracking and organizing data, and it often serves as an input interface for users. Automating the synchronization of this data to a database ensures that your system remains up-to-date and reduces the need for manual data entry.

To achieve this, you can use the **Google Sheets API** to access the data in a sheet and then write that data into your database (e.g., MySQL, MongoDB).

Example: Syncing Data from Google Sheets to a MySQL Database

1. **Set up Google Sheets API**:
   o Create a Google Cloud project and enable the **Google Sheets API**.
   o Create **OAuth credentials** to authenticate and access Google Sheets data.
2. **Install Required Packages**:

```bash
npm install googleapis mysql2
```

3. **Write Code to Fetch Data from Google Sheets and Insert into MySQL Database**:

```javascript
const { google } = require('googleapis');
const mysql = require('mysql2');

// Google Sheets API authentication
const sheets = google.sheets('v4');
const auth = new google.auth.GoogleAuth({
  keyFile: 'path/to/your/credentials.json', // Path to your Google API credentials
  scopes: ['https://www.googleapis.com/auth/spreadsheets.readonly'],
});

// Database connection
const db = mysql.createConnection({
  host: 'localhost',
  user: 'root',
  password: 'password',
  database: 'mydb'
});
```

```javascript
// Function to fetch data from Google Sheets
async function fetchDataFromSheet() {
    const client = await auth.getClient();
    const sheetId = 'your-google-sheet-id';
    const range = 'Sheet1!A1:C10'; // Adjust the
range as needed

    const res = await
sheets.spreadsheets.values.get({
        auth: client,
        spreadsheetId: sheetId,
        range: range,
    });

    const rows = res.data.values;
    if (rows.length) {
        console.log('Data from Google Sheets:',
rows);
        return rows;
    } else {
        console.log('No data found.');
        return [];
    }
}

// Function to sync data with MySQL
async function syncDataToDatabase() {
    const sheetData = await fetchDataFromSheet();
```

179

```
sheetData.forEach(row => {
  const [name, email, phone] = row;
  db.query(
    'INSERT INTO users (name, email, phone)
VALUES (?, ?, ?)',
    [name, email, phone],
    (err, results) => {
      if (err) {
        console.error('Error inserting data:',
err);
      } else {
        console.log('Inserted          user:',
results);
      }
    }
  );
});
}


// Start the sync process
syncDataToDatabase();
```

Explanation:

- **Google Sheets API**: We authenticate and connect to the Google Sheets API to fetch data from a specific range of the sheet.

- **MySQL Database**: The script then inserts the fetched data into a MySQL database, assuming you have a table `users` with columns `name`, `email`, and `phone`.

This script automates the process of synchronizing data from Google Sheets to your database. The synchronization process can be run at regular intervals or triggered by specific events.

Using APIs to Automate Data Exchange

APIs are a powerful way to exchange data between different services. By using **RESTful APIs**, you can send data from one service to another and automate the process of keeping data consistent across platforms.

Common API integration scenarios include:

- **Syncing data between Google Contacts and a CRM system**.
- **Pulling data from a payment processing system** (e.g., Stripe) into a database or other application.
- **Pushing data to third-party services** (e.g., sending marketing data to Mailchimp or Salesforce).

Most modern APIs follow a **REST** architecture, where each API request corresponds to one of the **CRUD** operations (Create, Read, Update, Delete).

Example: Automating Data Sync Between CRM and Google Contacts Using APIs

Let's say you want to sync contact information between your CRM system and **Google Contacts**. You can use the **Google People API** to manage contacts on Google Contacts.

1. **Set Up Google People API**:
   - Create a project in the Google Developer Console.
   - Enable the **Google People API**.
   - Set up OAuth credentials to allow access to the user's contacts.
2. **Install Required Libraries**:

bash

```
npm install googleapis
```

3. **Example Code to Sync CRM Data with Google Contacts**:

javascript

```
const { google } = require('googleapis');
const crmContacts = [
  { name: 'John Doe', email:
'john.doe@example.com', phone: '+1234567890' },
```

182

```
  { name: 'Jane Smith', email:
'jane.smith@example.com', phone: '+0987654321'
  },
];


// Google People API authentication
const people = google.people('v1');
const auth = new google.auth.GoogleAuth({
  keyFile: 'path/to/your/credentials.json',
  scopes:
['https://www.googleapis.com/auth/contacts'],
});


// Function to add contacts to Google Contacts
async function addContactsToGoogle() {
  const client = await auth.getClient();

  for (const crmContact of crmContacts) {
    const contact = {
      names: [{ givenName: crmContact.name }],
      emailAddresses: [{ value: crmContact.email
}],
      phoneNumbers: [{ value: crmContact.phone
}],
    };

    try {
      await people.people.createContact({
        auth: client,
```

183

```
      requestBody: contact,
   });
   console.log(`Contact    ${crmContact.name}
added to Google Contacts.`);
   } catch (error) {
   console.error(`Error              adding
${crmContact.name} to Google Contacts:`, error);
   }
  }
}


// Sync contacts from CRM to Google Contacts
addContactsToGoogle();
```

Explanation:

- This script uses the **Google People API** to add contacts to Google Contacts. It takes a set of contacts (in this case, CRM data), formats it into the required structure, and adds it to the Google Contacts.
- It uses OAuth credentials to authenticate the API requests and create new contacts on the user's Google account.

Real-World Example: Syncing a CRM System with Google Contacts

To automate syncing contacts between a CRM system and Google Contacts, you can set up a periodic task or webhook to trigger the

184

sync process whenever new data is available. For example, the sync process could be triggered:

- **Daily**: At a fixed time each day to ensure the CRM and Google Contacts are in sync.
- **Real-Time**: Whenever new contact data is added to the CRM (via an API webhook).

By automating the data synchronization process, you eliminate the need for manual data entry and ensure that your contact data is always up-to-date across platforms.

Conclusion

In this chapter, we covered **automating data synchronization** between platforms using JavaScript. We explored:

- **Synchronizing data from Google Sheets to a database**, enabling you to automatically move data from user-friendly interfaces to a central system.
- **Using APIs to automate data exchange**, including syncing data between a CRM system and Google Contacts.
- Real-world examples to demonstrate how automation can simplify processes and improve data consistency.

With JavaScript and its ecosystem of powerful libraries and APIs, automating data synchronization tasks has never been easier. Whether you're syncing Google Sheets with a database or integrating systems via APIs, these practices help streamline workflows and ensure data consistency across platforms.

CHAPTER 17

AUTOMATING FILE AND FOLDER MANAGEMENT

Automating File Organization (Sorting, Renaming, Moving Files)

In many applications, managing files and directories efficiently is crucial for organizing data, backups, and documents. Automating tasks like **sorting**, **renaming**, and **moving** files can save a lot of time, especially when dealing with large numbers of files. With **Node.js**, you can automate these processes using its built-in **fs** (file system) module, along with other utility libraries.

1. Sorting Files

Sorting files can involve organizing them based on criteria like:

- **File type (extension)**: Sorting by `.jpg`, `.pdf`, `.txt`, etc.
- **Date created/modified**: Sorting files by the creation or modification date.
- **Size**: Sorting by file size.

Example: Sorting Files by Extension

```
javascript
```

```
const fs = require('fs');
const path = require('path');

// Directory to scan
const directoryPath = './files';

// Read all files in the directory
fs.readdir(directoryPath, (err, files) => {
  if (err) {
    console.log('Error    reading    directory:',
err);
    return;
  }

  // Sort files by their extension
  const sortedFiles = files.sort((a, b) => {
    const extA = path.extname(a).toLowerCase();
    const extB = path.extname(b).toLowerCase();
    return extA.localeCompare(extB);   // Sort by
file extension
  });

  console.log('Sorted    files    by    extension:',
sortedFiles);
});
```

Explanation:

- **fs.readdir()**: Reads all the files in a specified directory.
- **path.extname()**: Extracts the file extension.
- **localeCompare()**: Compares strings and sorts them alphabetically (in this case, by file extension).

2. Renaming Files

Renaming files can help maintain organization, especially when working with files that have generic names (like `file1.txt`, `file2.txt`). Node.js provides the `fs.rename()` method to rename files programmatically.

Example: Renaming Files in a Directory

javascript

```
const fs = require('fs');
const path = require('path');

// Directory containing files to rename
const directoryPath = './files';

fs.readdir(directoryPath, (err, files) => {
  if (err) {
    console.log('Error   reading   directory:',
err);
    return;
  }
```

189

```
files.forEach((file, index) => {
  const oldPath = path.join(directoryPath,
file);
  const newFileName = `file_${index +
1}${path.extname(file)}`;    //    Renaming    to
'file_1.txt', 'file_2.jpg', etc.
  const newPath = path.join(directoryPath,
newFileName);

  // Rename the file
  fs.rename(oldPath, newPath, (err) => {
    if (err) {
      console.log('Error    renaming    file:',
err);
      return;
    }
    console.log(`Renamed       ${file}       to
${newFileName}`);
  });
});
```

Explanation:

- **path.join()**: Joins directory and file names to form the full file paths.
- **fs.rename()**: Renames the file to the new name.

190

- This script renames files in the specified directory, using a sequential naming scheme (file_1.txt, file_2.jpg, etc.).

3. Moving Files Between Directories

You may want to automatically move files to different directories based on their types, creation dates, or other criteria.

Example: Moving Files Based on File Type

javascript

```
const fs = require('fs');
const path = require('path');

// Directory to scan
const sourceDir = './files';
const destinationDir = './sorted_files';

// Ensure destination directory exists
fs.mkdirSync(destinationDir, { recursive: true
});

fs.readdir(sourceDir, (err, files) => {
  if (err) {
    console.log('Error      reading      source
directory:', err);
    return;
```

```
  }

  files.forEach((file) => {
    const filePath = path.join(sourceDir, file);
    const                    ext                =
path.extname(file).toLowerCase();
    const           destinationPath           =
path.join(destinationDir, ext, file);

    // Create subdirectory for file extension if
it doesn't exist
    fs.mkdirSync(path.dirname(destinationPath),
{ recursive: true });

    // Move the file
    fs.rename(filePath, destinationPath, (err)
=> {
      if (err) {
        console.log('Error moving file:', err);
        return;
      }
      console.log(`Moved      ${file}      to
${destinationPath}`);
    });
  });
});
```

Explanation:

- **fs.mkdirSync()**: Ensures that the destination subdirectories exist before moving files.
- **fs.rename()**: Moves the file from the source to the destination directory based on its file type (extension).

Using Node.js to Monitor and Automate File System Tasks

In addition to file manipulation, Node.js allows you to **monitor file changes** in real-time and automate responses to these changes. This can be done using the fs.watch() or chokidar library.

1. Using fs.watch() to Monitor File Changes

The fs.watch() function allows you to monitor a directory or file for changes, such as modifications, additions, or deletions.

Example: Monitoring File Changes in a Directory

javascript

```
const fs = require('fs');
const directoryPath = './files';

fs.watch(directoryPath, (eventType, filename) =>
{
  if (filename) {
    console.log(`${eventType} detected on file:
${filename}`);
```

193

```
    if (eventType === 'rename') {
      // Check if file was added or deleted
      if (fs.existsSync(path.join(directoryPath,
filename))) {
        console.log(`${filename}  was  added  or
renamed`);
      } else {
        console.log(`${filename} was deleted`);
      }
    }
  } else {
    console.log('No filename provided');
  }
});
```

Explanation:

- **fs.watch()**: Watches a specified directory for file changes.

- **eventType**: Indicates the type of change (rename or change).

- **fs.existsSync()**: Checks if the file exists after a rename event to determine whether it was added or deleted.

194

2. Using `chokidar` for More Reliable Monitoring

`chokidar` is a third-party library that offers more reliable and efficient file system watching. It can handle a broader range of file system events and works better across platforms.

Installing `chokidar`:

bash

npm install chokidar

Example: Monitoring File Additions Using `chokidar`

javascript

```
const chokidar = require('chokidar');

const watcher = chokidar.watch('./files', { persistent: true });

watcher.on('add', (path) => {
  console.log(`File ${path} has been added.`);
});

watcher.on('change', (path) => {
  console.log(`File ${path} has been changed.`);
});
```

```
watcher.on('unlink', (path) => {
  console.log(`File ${path} has been removed.`);
});
```

Explanation:

- **chokidar.watch()**: Watches the directory for file changes.
- **add, change, unlink**: Events that are triggered when a file is added, modified, or deleted, respectively.

Real-World Example: Automating a Backup System

A common real-world task for automating file management is creating a **backup system**. We can automate the backup of files from one directory to another, either by ing files or compressing them.

Example: Automating File Backup with Node.js

javascript

```
const fs = require('fs');
const path = require('path');
const zlib = require('zlib');
const tar = require('tar');

// Source and destination directories
const sourceDir = './files';
```

```
const backupDir = './backups';

// Function to backup files
function backupFiles() {
  const               date           =            new
Date().toISOString().split('T')[0];       //   Get
current date
  const              backupFileName            =
`backup_${date}.tar.gz`;
  const  backupFilePath  =  path.join(backupDir,
backupFileName);

  // Create a tarball of the source directory and
compress it
  tar.c(
    {
      gzip: true,
      file: backupFilePath,
    },
    [sourceDir]
  ).then(() => {
    console.log(`Backup                     created:
${backupFilePath}`);
  }).catch(err => {
    console.log('Error creating backup:', err);
  });
}

// Schedule backup every 24 hours
```

```
setInterval(backupFiles, 24 * 60 * 60 * 1000);
// 24 hours in milliseconds
```

Explanation:

- **tar.c()**: Creates a compressed .tar.gz archive of the source directory.
- **setInterval()**: Automates the backup process to run every 24 hours.

This system creates daily backups of the files directory and stores them in the backups directory with the current date.

Conclusion

In this chapter, we explored how to **automate file and folder management** with Node.js. We covered:

- **File organization tasks** like sorting, renaming, and moving files using the **fs** module.
- **Monitoring file system changes** using fs.watch() and **chokidar**.
- A **real-world example** of creating an automated **backup system** to back up files using compression and scheduled tasks.

By automating file management tasks, you save time, reduce human error, and ensure better organization and backup of your data. With Node.js and its built-in file system tools, you can automate and streamline many file-related tasks in your applications.

CHAPTER 18

HANDLING AUTOMATION ERRORS AND FAILURES

Best Practices for Error Handling in Automation Scripts

Error handling is an essential part of automation. When building automation scripts, it's crucial to anticipate potential errors and handle them gracefully. Without proper error handling, automation processes can fail silently, leading to incomplete tasks or undetected issues.

Here are some **best practices** for handling errors in automation scripts:

1. Use Try-Catch Blocks for Synchronous Code

For synchronous code, use **try-catch** blocks to catch exceptions and handle errors effectively.

Example:

```javascript

try {
```

```
  // Code that may throw an error
  const result = riskyFunction();
  console.log('Success:', result);
} catch (error) {
  console.error('An        error        occurred:',
error.message);
  // Handle the error (e.g., retry, alert user,
log the error)
}
```

- **try**: Contains the code that may throw an error.
- **catch**: Handles any errors that occur within the try block.

2. Use Promises and Catch Errors in Asynchronous Code

For asynchronous operations, such as database queries, file I/O, or network requests, use .catch() to handle errors in **Promises**.

Example with Promises:

javascript

```
fetch('https://example.com')
  .then(response => response.json())
  .then(data => console.log(data))
  .catch(error => {
    console.error('Error      fetching      data:',
error.message);
```

```
    // Handle the error (e.g., retry or alert the
user)
  });
```

3. Handle Errors in Async/Await Syntax

For **async/await** syntax, use `try-catch` blocks around `await` expressions to catch errors in asynchronous code.

Example with Async/Await:

javascript

```
async function fetchData() {
  try {
    const          response          =          await
fetch('https://example.com');
    const data = await response.json();
    console.log(data);
  } catch (error) {
    console.error('Error     fetching     data:',
error.message);
    // Handle the error (e.g., retry, alert the
user)
  }
}


fetchData();
```

- **try**: Executes the asynchronous code.

- **catch**: Catches errors if the promise rejects or an exception occurs during the execution of the `await` expression.

4. Fail Gracefully and Provide Useful Feedback

When an error occurs, provide meaningful feedback to the user or system. Don't just print generic error messages like "An error occurred." Provide details, including:

- The nature of the error.
- Suggested steps for recovery or troubleshooting.

Example:

javascript

```
try {
  // Attempting to process data
  processData();
} catch (error) {
  console.error('Data processing failed: ',
error.message);
  // Retry or send a notification with helpful
details
}
```

5. Avoid Silent Failures

Ensure that your automation script doesn't fail silently. Always log errors or send notifications when something goes wrong. Never leave an automation process running without error feedback.

Logging and Monitoring Automation Processes

Logging and monitoring are critical to understanding how your automation scripts are performing. Proper logging helps you track the execution flow, capture unexpected errors, and analyze the state of the system.

1. Use Structured Logging

Use structured logging where logs include relevant metadata like timestamps, error codes, and specific context to make troubleshooting easier. Use libraries like **Winston** or **Pino** for more advanced logging.

Installing Winston:

```bash
bash
```

```bash
npm install winston
```

Example: Using Winston for Structured Logging

```
javascript

const winston = require('winston');

// Create a logger
const logger = winston.createLogger({
  level: 'info',
  transports: [
    new winston.transports.Console({ format:
winston.format.simple() }),
    new winston.transports.File({ filename:
'app.log' })
  ]
});

// Logging examples
logger.info('Automation script started');
logger.warn('Warning: Something might go
wrong');
logger.error('Error occurred during the
process');
```

Explanation:

- **info()**: Logs general information.
- **warn()**: Logs warnings.
- **error()**: Logs error messages.

You can configure Winston to log in different formats (e.g., JSON, simple text), and store logs in files or send them to remote servers for centralized logging.

2. Monitoring Tools

To track automation processes in real-time, use **monitoring tools** such as:

- **Prometheus** for collecting and querying metrics.
- **Grafana** for visualizing and analyzing logs.
- **Datadog**, **New Relic**, or **Sentry** for application performance monitoring and error tracking.

These tools allow you to track metrics like:

- Execution time of tasks.
- Number of successful and failed operations.
- Resource consumption (CPU, memory).

Example: Monitoring Execution Time with Prometheus

```javascript
const prometheus = require('prom-client');
const            collectDefaultMetrics            =
prometheus.collectDefaultMetrics;
```

```
// Collect default metrics (CPU usage, memory
usage, etc.)
collectDefaultMetrics();

// Custom metric to track the execution time of
a function
const      executionDuration      =      new
prometheus.Histogram({
  name: 'automation_execution_duration_seconds',
  help: 'Duration of automation tasks in
seconds',
  buckets: [0.1, 0.5, 1, 2, 5, 10]
});

// Measure function execution time
async function task() {
  const end = executionDuration.startTimer();
  await someAsyncOperation();
  end();
}
```

Explanation:

- **prom-client** is a popular library for exporting metrics to Prometheus.
- **Histogram** tracks the duration of tasks and generates metrics that can be visualized in monitoring systems.

3. Sending Alerts and Notifications

When a failure occurs or a critical event is logged, you should send alerts or notifications to the system administrator or the team responsible for monitoring.

You can integrate alerts with tools like **Slack**, **email**, or **SMS**.

Example: Sending Slack Notifications on Errors

```javascript
const axios = require('axios');

// Send a message to Slack on error
function sendSlackNotification(message) {

axios.post('https://slack.com/api/chat.postMessage', {
    text: message,
    channel: '#alerts',
    token: 'your-slack-api-token'
  }).then(response => {
    console.log('Notification sent to Slack');
  }).catch(error => {
    console.error('Error     sending     Slack
notification:', error.message);
  });
}
```

208

```
// Usage
sendSlackNotification('Critical   failure   in   the
automation process');
```

Real-World Example: Debugging a Failed Deployment Automation Script

Imagine you've set up an automation script that deploys an application to a server. However, the deployment fails, and the script doesn't provide sufficient error information. To debug this, follow these steps:

1. Add Logging for Deployment Steps

You should start by adding detailed logs for each step in your deployment process. For instance, log the start and end times for each step and any errors that occur.

Example: Enhanced Deployment Script with Logging

```javascript
const winston = require('winston');
const exec = require('child_process').exec;

const logger = winston.createLogger({
  level: 'info',
```

209

```javascript
  transports: [
    new winston.transports.Console(),
    new    winston.transports.File({    filename:
'deployment.log' })
  ]
});

function deployApp() {
  logger.info('Deployment started');

  // Run build step
  exec('npm run build', (error, stdout, stderr)
=> {
    if (error) {
      logger.error('Build   step   failed:   '   +
error.message);
      return;
    }
    logger.info('Build completed successfully');
  });

  // Run deployment step
  exec('pm2  restart  my-app',  (error,  stdout,
stderr) => {
    if (error) {
      logger.error('Deployment   failed:   '   +
error.message);
      return;
    }
```

```
    logger.info('App deployed successfully');
  });
}
```

```
deployApp();
```

Explanation:

- **winston logger**: We use it to log success and failure messages.
- **exec()**: Executes shell commands, and we log both the standard output (stdout) and any errors.

2. Analyze Logs

After the script fails, analyze the logs:

- **Look for error messages**: If a command fails, the error message will give you clues (e.g., missing dependencies, network issues).
- **Check timestamps**: Ensure the process is executing as expected, and identify where it might be hanging or failing.

3. Add Alerts for Critical Failures

To ensure timely response to failures, add automated notifications. In this case, you could use **Slack notifications** (as shown in the earlier example) to alert the team when the deployment fails.

211

Conclusion

In this chapter, we covered essential concepts for **error handling**, **logging**, and **monitoring** in automation scripts. We:

- Discussed best practices for error handling in both synchronous and asynchronous code.
- Explored logging techniques and introduced **Winston** for structured logging.
- Learned how to monitor automation processes with tools like **Prometheus** and **Slack** for notifications.
- Walked through a **real-world example** of debugging a failed deployment automation script by improving logging and adding alerts.

By implementing proper error handling, logging, and monitoring, you can significantly improve the reliability of your automation scripts and quickly identify and resolve issues. These practices are essential for maintaining smooth and efficient automated workflows.

CHAPTER 19

AUTOMATING SCHEDULING AND CRON JOBS

Setting Up Scheduled Tasks with Node.js

In many applications, automating **scheduled tasks** can help maintain processes that need to run at specific intervals. These tasks could include actions like sending email notifications, generating reports, cleaning up files, or backing up data.

Cron jobs are a popular way to schedule tasks on Unix-based systems (like Linux and macOS), and in the context of **Node.js**, they can be automated using libraries like **node-cron** or built-in features like **setInterval** and **setTimeout**.

1. What is a Cron Job?

A **cron job** is a time-based job scheduler that runs tasks at specified intervals. For example, you might want to run a backup script every night at midnight or clean temporary files every hour. Cron jobs are configured using cron expressions, a special syntax to specify the timing of the task.

A **cron expression** consists of five fields:

```lua

* * * * *
| | | | |
| | | | |
| |\| | +-- Day of week (0-7) (Sunday=0 or 7)
| | | +---- Month (1-12)
| | +------ Day of month (1-31)
| +-------- Hour (0-23)
+---------- Minute (0-59)
```

Using Libraries Like node-cron for Recurring Jobs

In Node.js, you can use the **node-cron** library to set up cron jobs that run at specific intervals, similar to using cron on a Unix system.

1. Installing node-cron

```bash

npm install node-cron
```
2. Setting Up a Basic Cron Job with node-cron

node-cron allows you to easily schedule tasks by using cron expressions. Let's set up a simple job that runs every minute:

```javascript

```

```
const cron = require('node-cron');

// Schedule a task to run every minute
cron.schedule('* * * * *', () => {
  console.log('This task runs every minute');
});
```

Explanation:

- **cron.schedule()**: The schedule() method accepts a cron expression and a callback function. The callback runs when the scheduled time is met.
- **Cron expression**: ' * * * * * ' means "run every minute".

3. Scheduling Recurring Jobs

You can use **node-cron** to schedule recurring tasks such as:

- Backing up data daily.
- Sending email reminders every week.
- Cleaning up old log files every month.

For instance, to schedule a task to run every day at midnight:

```
javascript
```

```
cron.schedule('0 0 * * *', () => {
```

215

```
console.log('Running task at midnight every
day');
});
```

Explanation:

- The cron expression '0 0 * * *' means the task will run at **midnight every day**.

4. Handling Task Failures and Timeouts

Sometimes, tasks may fail due to network errors, server downtime, or other unforeseen issues. In such cases, it's essential to handle errors gracefully. You can use try-catch blocks within your cron jobs to catch exceptions or handle timeouts.

```javascript
cron.schedule('0 0 * * *', async () => {
  try {
    console.log('Running daily backup...');
    // Simulate the backup process
    await runBackup();
  } catch (error) {
    console.error('Backup            failed:',
error.message);
  }
});
```

Real-World Example: Automating Nightly Data Backups

Automating **data backups** is one of the most common use cases for scheduled tasks. In this real-world example, we'll set up a **nightly backup** of files or database data.

1. Requirements

- Backup files from a source directory to a destination directory every night.
- Use a cron job to automate the backup process.
- Ensure proper logging to track success and failure.

2. Automating the Backup Process

Here's how you can set up a cron job to automate nightly backups of a directory:

1. **Install Necessary Packages**

For this example, we will use the `fs` module for file system operations and the `node-cron` library for scheduling.

bash

```
npm install node-cron
```

2. **Backup Script**

217

```javascript

const cron = require('node-cron');
const fs = require('fs');
const path = require('path');
const { exec } = require('child_process');

// Source and destination directories for backup
const sourceDir = './data';
const backupDir = './backups';

// Function to  files from source to destination
function backupFiles() {
  const             date              =            new
Date().toISOString().split('T')[0];   // Get the
current date
  const backupFolderName = `backup_${date}`;
  const    backupPath    =    path.join(backupDir,
backupFolderName);

  // Create backup directory if it doesn't exist
  if (!fs.existsSync(backupPath)) {
    fs.mkdirSync(backupPath, { recursive: true
});
  }

  // Use exec to run the 'cp' command to  files
  exec(`cp  -r  ${sourceDir}/*  ${backupPath}`,
(error, stdout, stderr) => {
```

```
    if (error) {
      console.error(`Error     during     backup:
${error.message}`);
      return;
    }
    if (stderr) {
      console.error(`stderr: ${stderr}`);
      return;
    }
    console.log(`Backup   completed   successfully
at ${backupPath}`);
  });
}


// Schedule the backup to run every night at 2 AM
cron.schedule('0 2 * * *', backupFiles);
```

Explanation:

- **backupFiles()** : This function performs the file backup.
  It creates a backup folder with the current date as the
  folder name and uses the cp command to the files from
  the sourceDir to the backupDir.

- **cron.schedule('0 2 * * *', backupFiles)** : This
  schedules the backup process to run every day at **2 AM**.
  The cron expression '0 2 * * *' means the task will
  run at 2:00 AM daily.

219

3. Enhancing the Backup System

For a more robust system, you can include features like:

- **Compression**: Compress files into a `.tar.gz` archive to save space.
- **Email Notifications**: Send an email notification if the backup fails or completes successfully.
- **Database Backups**: Automate the backup of databases like MySQL, MongoDB, etc., in addition to file backups.

Example: Sending Email Notifications

You can integrate **NodeMailer** to send an email when the backup completes or fails.

```javascript
const nodemailer = require('nodemailer');

// Function to send email notification
function sendEmailNotification(subject, message) {
  const transporter = nodemailer.createTransport({
    service: 'gmail',
    auth: {
      user: 'your-email@gmail.com',
      pass: 'your-email-password',
```

```javascript
    },
  });

  const mailOptions = {
    from: 'your-email@gmail.com',
    to: 'recipient@example.com',
    subject: subject,
    text: message,
  };

  transporter.sendMail(mailOptions,        (error,
info) => {
    if (error) {
      return console.log('Error sending email:',
error);
    }
    console.log('Email sent:', info.response);
  });
}

// Modify the backup function to send email after
completion
function backupFiles() {
  const         date         =         new
Date().toISOString().split('T')[0];
  const backupFolderName = `backup_${date}`;
  const    backupPath    =    path.join(backupDir,
backupFolderName);
```

```
  if (!fs.existsSync(backupPath)) {
    fs.mkdirSync(backupPath, { recursive: true
});
  }


  exec(`cp -r ${sourceDir}/* ${backupPath}`,
(error, stdout, stderr) => {
    if (error) {
      sendEmailNotification('Backup      Failed',
`Backup failed with error: ${error.message}`);
      return;
    }
    if (stderr) {
      sendEmailNotification('Backup      Warning',
`Backup completed with warnings: ${stderr}`);
      return;
    }
    sendEmailNotification('Backup      Completed',
`Backup       successfully      completed      at
${backupPath}`);
  });
}


cron.schedule('0 2 * * *', backupFiles);
```

Conclusion

In this chapter, we explored how to **automate scheduling and cron jobs** using **Node.js**. We:

- **Learned how to set up cron jobs** using the **node-cron** library to schedule recurring tasks.
- **Created a real-world example**: Automating a nightly data backup system, including backup scripts, logging, and email notifications.
- **Improved the backup process** by adding email alerts, error handling, and the option to compress backups.

By automating recurring tasks like backups, you can ensure data integrity, reduce the risk of human error, and improve the overall reliability of your system.

CHAPTER 20

SECURITY CONSIDERATIONS IN AUTOMATION

Securing Your Automation Scripts

When automating tasks, security should be one of the top priorities. Automation scripts often interact with sensitive systems, databases, and APIs. If not secured properly, they could expose critical information or provide an entry point for attackers. Here are key principles for securing your automation scripts:

1. Limit Permissions

Principle of Least Privilege (PoLP): Ensure that automation scripts have the **minimum level of access** required to perform their tasks. Avoid using accounts with full administrative privileges unless absolutely necessary.

- **Use service accounts** with only the permissions needed for the automation task.
- **Restrict API access** to only the necessary endpoints or data.

2. Avoid Hardcoding Sensitive Information

Never hardcode sensitive information (such as passwords, API keys, or tokens) directly in your scripts. Hardcoding these values in your code exposes them to anyone with access to your source code, potentially leading to unauthorized access.

3. Secure Authentication

If your automation script needs to authenticate to external services (e.g., APIs or databases), always prefer secure methods like:

- **OAuth2**: Use token-based authentication for APIs instead of embedding credentials.
- **Environment variables**: Store sensitive data like API keys or passwords in environment variables instead of hardcoding them in scripts.
- **SSH Keys**: Use SSH keys for authenticating to remote servers instead of passwords.

4. Logging and Monitoring

Set up **logging and monitoring** to detect any suspicious activity. Ensure that logs are secure and don't expose sensitive information (e.g., passwords, tokens).

- **Use secure logging mechanisms** to capture and store logs in a centralized, secure location.

- Monitor for unusual patterns (e.g., failed authentication attempts, unexpected access).

5. Encrypt Sensitive Data

If your automation scripts process sensitive data (e.g., personal information or payment data), ensure that the data is encrypted both at rest and in transit.

- **Use HTTPS** for all API calls to protect data in transit.
- **Encrypt data at rest** using tools like **AES** or **RSA** for sensitive data stored in files or databases.

Best Practices for Handling Sensitive Data (API Keys, Passwords)

Sensitive data, such as API keys, passwords, or access tokens, must be handled securely to prevent unauthorized access to your systems. Here are the best practices for managing sensitive data in automation scripts:

1. Use Environment Variables

Instead of hardcoding sensitive information into your scripts, store it in **environment variables**. Environment variables keep sensitive data outside your codebase and allow you to manage it securely.

Example: Storing API Key in an Environment Variable

1. **Create a .env file** to store environment variables:

bash

```
# .env file
API_KEY=your-api-key-here
DATABASE_PASSWORD=your-database-password-here
```

2. **Load the environment variables in your Node.js script**:

bash

```
npm install dotenv
javascript
```

```
// Load environment variables from .env file
require('dotenv').config();

// Access sensitive data using process.env
const apiKey = process.env.API_KEY;
const            dbPassword            =
process.env.DATABASE_PASSWORD;

console.log('API Key:', apiKey);
```

227

- The **dotenv** library loads environment variables from a
  `.env` file, making it easier to manage sensitive data
  securely.

2. Use Secrets Management Services

For added security, use **secrets management services** like **AWS Secrets Manager**, **HashiCorp Vault**, or **Azure Key Vault**. These services store and manage sensitive information like API keys and passwords securely, and they provide mechanisms for rotating secrets.

Example: Using AWS Secrets Manager

javascript

```javascript
const AWS = require('aws-sdk');
const secretName = 'mySecret';

const client = new AWS.SecretsManager({
  region: 'us-east-1'
});

async function getSecret() {
  try {
    const data = await client.getSecretValue({
SecretId: secretName }).promise();
    if (data.SecretString) {
```

```
    const            secret            =
JSON.parse(data.SecretString);
    console.log('Secret:', secret);
  }
 } catch (err) {
    console.log('Error   retrieving   secret:',
err);
  }
}


getSecret();
```

- **AWS Secrets Manager** stores and retrieves secrets like API keys, passwords, and other credentials in a secure way.

3. Rotate Secrets Regularly

Periodically rotate your **API keys, passwords**, and **access tokens** to reduce the risk of compromise. Many secrets management systems can automatically rotate secrets on a schedule.

4. Avoid Logging Sensitive Information

Do not log sensitive information such as passwords, API keys, or tokens in your logs. If a log is exposed or leaked, it could provide attackers with sensitive data. Always ensure that logs are sanitized before being written.

Example: Logging Without Sensitive Information

```javascript
const password = 'my-secret-password';
const userInput = 'Sensitive info';

// Incorrect: Logging sensitive information
console.log(`User password: ${password}`);  // Do not log sensitive data

// Correct: Masking sensitive data in logs
console.log(`User input: ${userInput.replace(/./g, '*')}`);  // Masking sensitive info
```

Real-World Example: Automating Login Without Exposing Credentials

One common automation task is logging into a website or service programmatically. However, it's critical to avoid hardcoding **user credentials** in the script.

1. Automating Login with OAuth2 (Instead of Hardcoding Credentials)

Instead of hardcoding a username and password, you can automate login using **OAuth2**. OAuth2 allows you to authenticate securely using tokens, eliminating the need to expose passwords in your automation script.

Example: Automating Login to Google API using OAuth2

1. **Install the required libraries**:

bash

```
npm install googleapis google-auth-library
```

2. **Set up OAuth2 authentication**:

javascript

```
const { google } = require('googleapis');
const { OAuth2Client } = require('google-auth-library');

// OAuth2 credentials
const oauth2Client = new OAuth2Client(
  'your-client-id',
  'your-client-secret',
  'your-redirect-url'
);

// Get the OAuth2 authorization URL
const authUrl = oauth2Client.generateAuthUrl({
  access_type: 'offline',
```

231

```
  scope:
['https://www.googleapis.com/auth/drive.file']
});

// Redirect the user to the authorization URL
console.log('Authorize this app by visiting this
url:', authUrl);

// After the user grants access, retrieve the
authorization code
// Exchange the authorization code for tokens
async function getTokens(authCode) {
  const      {      tokens     }     =      await
oauth2Client.getToken(authCode);
  oauth2Client.setCredentials(tokens);
  console.log('Tokens:', tokens);
}

// Example: Getting tokens using an authorization
code
getTokens('authorization-code-here');
```

Explanation:

- **OAuth2Client**: This class handles the OAuth2 flow, where the user is prompted to grant access to their Google account.

- **Access tokens**: Once the user authorizes the app, the **authorization code** is exchanged for **access tokens**. These tokens are then used for subsequent API calls.

By using OAuth2, we avoid directly handling and storing user credentials (username/password), and instead use secure tokens to authenticate with external services.

2. Using Environment Variables for Credentials

To ensure credentials are not hardcoded in the script, store sensitive information like **client IDs** and **client secrets** in environment variables.

1. **Create a .env file**:

bash

```
# .env
GOOGLE_CLIENT_ID=your-client-id
GOOGLE_CLIENT_SECRET=your-client-secret
GOOGLE_REDIRECT_URL=your-redirect-url
```

2. **Use dotenv to load credentials securely**:

javascript

```
require('dotenv').config();
```

```
const clientId = process.env.GOOGLE_CLIENT_ID;
const           clientSecret            =
process.env.GOOGLE_CLIENT_SECRET;
const              redirectUrl          =
process.env.GOOGLE_REDIRECT_URL;

const oauth2Client = new OAuth2Client(clientId,
clientSecret, redirectUrl);
```

By using environment variables, you keep sensitive information out of the codebase and ensure that credentials are handled securely.

Conclusion

In this chapter, we explored **security considerations** when automating tasks, including:

- **Best practices** for handling sensitive data, such as **API keys**, **passwords**, and **access tokens**.
- The importance of **secure authentication methods** like **OAuth2** instead of hardcoding credentials.
- How to use **environment variables** and **secrets management services** for secure data handling.
- A **real-world example** of automating login without exposing credentials using OAuth2 and **Google APIs**.

By following these security best practices, you can ensure that your automation scripts are both secure and efficient, safeguarding sensitive data and reducing the risk of unauthorized access.

CHAPTER 21

AUTOMATING FILE DOWNLOADS AND UPLOADS

Using JavaScript for Downloading and Uploading Files Automatically

Automating file downloads and uploads is an essential part of many workflows, especially for applications that interact with external systems, APIs, or cloud services. Whether you need to download data from a server, or upload files to a storage service, JavaScript provides several ways to automate these processes using both **client-side** (browser-based) and **server-side** (Node.js) methods.

1. Automating File Downloads

To automate the downloading of files using **Node.js**, you typically work with modules like **https** or **axios** to send HTTP requests and download the files to your local file system.

Example: Using Node.js and axios for File Downloads

To download a file, you can use the `axios` library, which makes it easier to send HTTP requests and handle responses, including file streams.

1. **Install axios**:

bash

```
npm install axios
```

2. **Downloading a File with axios**:

javascript

```
const axios = require('axios');
const fs = require('fs');
const path = require('path');

// URL of the file to be downloaded
const                    fileUrl                    =
'https://example.com/sample.csv';
const fileName = 'sample.csv';
const filePath = path.join(__dirname, fileName);

// Download the file
axios({
  method: 'get',
  url: fileUrl,
  responseType: 'stream',
})
```

```
    .then(response => {
      const            writer           =
fs.createWriteStream(filePath);
      response.data.pipe(writer);
      writer.on('finish', () => {
        console.log(`File       downloaded       to
${filePath}`);
      });
      writer.on('error', (err) => {
        console.error('Error    downloading    the
file:', err);
      });
    })
    .catch(error => {
      console.error('Error:', error.message);
    });
```

Explanation:

- **axios**: Sends an HTTP request to download the file.
- **responseType: 'stream'**: Streams the file data from the server.
- **fs.createWriteStream()**: Creates a writable stream to save the file on the local file system.

This code automates the download of a file (in this case, a CSV file) and saves it to the local directory.

2. Automating File Uploads

Similarly, you can automate file uploads using **Node.js**. Typically, file uploads are done via HTTP POST requests, sending files to an API or web server.

Example: Using `axios` to Upload a File

1. **Install Form-Data (for multipart/form-data):**

bash

```
npm install form-data
```

2. **Uploading a File with `axios`:**

javascript

```
const axios = require('axios');
const fs = require('fs');
const FormData = require('form-data');

// File path to upload
const filePath = './sample.csv';

// Prepare form data for upload
const form = new FormData();
form.append('file',
fs.createReadStream(filePath));
```

239

```javascript
// Define upload URL
const uploadUrl = 'https://example.com/upload';

// Send POST request to upload the file
axios.post(uploadUrl, form, {
  headers: {
    ...form.getHeaders(),
  },
})
  .then(response => {
    console.log('File  uploaded  successfully:',
response.data);
  })
  .catch(error => {
    console.error('Error  uploading  the  file:',
error.message);
  });
```

Explanation:

- **FormData**: Creates a form to send the file as `multipart/form-data`.
- **fs.createReadStream()**: Reads the file to be uploaded.
- **axios.post()**: Sends the file to the server.

This code automates uploading a file to a server endpoint and handles the necessary HTTP request and headers.

Automating the Processing of File-Based Data

Automating the processing of downloaded or uploaded files is a common requirement in data-centric applications. For example, you might download a CSV file, parse its contents, process the data, and save the results to a database.

1. Automating CSV File Processing

CSV files are commonly used to store tabular data, and automating the processing of such files can help in scenarios like importing data from external sources, generating reports, or updating records in a database.

To process CSV files, you can use the **csv-parser** or **papaparse** library in Node.js.

Install csv-parser:

```bash
bash
```

```bash
npm install csv-parser
```

Example: Processing a CSV File in Node.js

```javascript
javascript
```

```javascript
const fs = require('fs');
```

241

```
const path = require('path');
const csv = require('csv-parser');

// Path to the downloaded CSV file
const      filePath    =      path.join(__dirname,
'sample.csv');

// Array to store processed data
const processedData = [];

// Function to process the CSV file
fs.createReadStream(filePath)
  .pipe(csv())
  .on('data', (row) => {
    // Process each row of data
    console.log(row); // Each  row  is  an  object
with key-value pairs
    processedData.push(row);
  })
  .on('end', () => {
    console.log('CSV           file          processed
successfully!');
    console.log('Processed                   data:',
processedData);
    // Here,  you  can  further  process  the  data,
save  it  to  a  database,  or  use  it  for  reporting
  })
  .on('error', (err) => {
```

```
    console.error('Error processing the file:',
err);
  });
```

Explanation:

- **csv-parser**: Parses the CSV file line by line.
- **fs.createReadStream()**: Streams the CSV file for processing.
- **on('data')**: Captures each row of data from the CSV and processes it.
- **on('end')**: Executes when the file is completely processed.

Once the data is processed, you can save it to a database, generate reports, or use it for other tasks.

2. Automating JSON File Processing

You might also need to process JSON files. JSON is a popular data format for exchanging structured data between services.

Example: Processing JSON Files

```javascript
const fs = require('fs');

// Path to the downloaded JSON file
```

```
const filePath = './data.json';

// Function to process the JSON file
fs.readFile(filePath, 'utf8', (err, data) => {
  if (err) {
    console.error('Error  reading  JSON  file:',
err);
    return;
  }

  // Parse the JSON data
  const jsonData = JSON.parse(data);

  // Process the data (e.g., filter, update, or
save to database)
  console.log('Data processed:', jsonData);
});
```

Explanation:

- **fs.readFile()**: Reads the JSON file.
- **JSON.parse()**: Converts the JSON string into a JavaScript object for processing.

244

Real-World Example: Automatically Downloading and Processing CSV Files

Let's consider a real-world example where you need to automate the download of a CSV file containing sales data, process it to calculate total sales, and then store the results in a database.

1. Automating the Download and Processing of CSV Data

1. **Install the required libraries**:

bash

```
npm install axios csv-parser mysql2
```

2. **Automating the download, processing, and saving of CSV data**:

javascript

```javascript
const axios = require('axios');
const fs = require('fs');
const csv = require('csv-parser');
const mysql = require('mysql2');
const path = require('path');

// URL of the CSV file
const fileUrl = 'https://example.com/sales-data.csv';
```

```javascript
const fileName = 'sales-data.csv';
const filePath = path.join(__dirname, fileName);

// Database connection
const db = mysql.createConnection({
  host: 'localhost',
  user: 'root',
  password: 'password',
  database: 'sales_db'
});

// Step 1: Download the CSV file
axios({
  method: 'get',
  url: fileUrl,
  responseType: 'stream',
})
  .then(response => {
    const                  writer         =
fs.createWriteStream(filePath);
    response.data.pipe(writer);
    writer.on('finish', () => {
      console.log('CSV      file      downloaded
successfully.');

      // Step 2: Process the downloaded CSV file
      let totalSales = 0;
      fs.createReadStream(filePath)
        .pipe(csv())
```

```
    .on('data', (row) => {
    const          saleAmount          =
parseFloat(row.amount); // Assuming "amount" is
a column in the CSV
    totalSales += saleAmount;
    })
    .on('end', () => {
    console.log('CSV    file    processed
successfully!');
    console.log('Total          Sales:',
totalSales);


    // Step 3: Save the processed data to
the database
    db.query('INSERT  INTO  sales_summary
(total_sales) VALUES (?)', [totalSales], (err,
results) => {
        if (err) {
        console.error('Error  saving  data
to the database:', err);
        } else {
        console.log('Sales  summary  saved
to the database:', results);
        }
      });
    })
    .on('error', (err) => {
    console.error('Error  processing  CSV
file:', err);
```

```
      });
    });
  })
  .catch(error => {
    console.error('Error   downloading   the   CSV
file:', error.message);
    });
  });
```

Explanation:

- **axios**: Downloads the CSV file from the provided URL.
- **csv-parser**: Processes the CSV file row by row and sums up the sales data.
- **MySQL**: The calculated total sales are saved into the database for further analysis or reporting.

This example demonstrates how to automate the entire workflow of downloading, processing, and storing data, which could be part of a nightly data processing pipeline.

Conclusion

In this chapter, we explored how to automate the process of **downloading** and **uploading** files using **Node.js**. We covered:

- Using **axios** to download and upload files programmatically.

- Automating the processing of **file-based data** such as **CSV** and **JSON** files.

- A **real-world example** where we automated the process of downloading a CSV file, processing its contents, and saving the results to a database.

By leveraging JavaScript and its ecosystem of libraries, you can automate file management tasks efficiently, allowing you to focus on more important aspects of your application while ensuring that data is processed and stored correctly.

CHAPTER 22

AUTOMATING SOCIAL MEDIA MANAGEMENT

Using JavaScript for Social Media Post Automation

In today's world, businesses and individuals often use social media to reach their audience, build relationships, and stay relevant. Social media management can become a time-consuming task, but **JavaScript** offers powerful tools and libraries to **automate social media posts**, manage accounts, and perform routine actions without manual intervention.

Social media platforms like **Twitter**, **Facebook**, and **Instagram** provide **APIs** that can be used to automate tasks such as posting updates, responding to messages, or even scheduling posts for later.

1. Benefits of Automating Social Media Management

- **Time-Saving**: Automate routine tasks like posting at specific times, responding to users, and following/unfollowing.

- **Consistency**: Post regularly without worrying about time zones or forgetting to share updates.
- **Engagement**: Automate responses to frequently asked questions or customer inquiries.
- **Data Collection**: Automatically collect data like user engagement, comments, or mentions for analysis.

2. Social Media APIs for Automation

Most social media platforms offer APIs that allow developers to automate tasks. These APIs provide methods to interact programmatically with the platform, enabling the following actions:

- **Twitter API**: Post tweets, reply to tweets, and like tweets.
- **Facebook Graph API**: Post status updates, retrieve user data, and manage pages.
- **Instagram API**: Post photos, like posts, and comment.

Each platform has its own authentication mechanism (typically **OAuth2**), so be sure to review their documentation to get the appropriate credentials.

Scheduling Posts and Automating Responses

Social media platforms generally provide methods to schedule posts or automate responses. To build an automated social media management system, you need the following components:

- **API Integration**: Use official APIs to interact with platforms.
- **Scheduling**: Automatically schedule posts for specific times (for example, using `node-cron`).
- **Automating Responses**: Set up automated responses for comments, messages, or mentions.

1. Scheduling Social Media Posts

Scheduling posts at specific times or intervals is a key feature of social media automation. You can achieve this by using **cron jobs** or a task scheduler like **node-cron** in conjunction with the social media API to post content at predefined times.

Example: Automating Twitter Posts Using Node.js

To automate posting on Twitter, you'll need to use **Twitter API** along with a Node.js package called `twit`. Here's how to set up Twitter automation:

1. Install the `twit` package:

```bash
npm install twit
```

2. Twitter Developer Access:

- Go to Twitter Developer to create an application.
- Obtain **API Key**, **API Secret Key**, **Access Token**, and **Access Token Secret**.

3. Automating Twitter Posts

```javascript
const Twit = require('twit');
const cron = require('node-cron');

// Set up Twitter API credentials
const T = new Twit({
  consumer_key: 'your-api-key',
  consumer_secret: 'your-api-secret',
  access_token: 'your-access-token',
  access_token_secret:       'your-access-token-
secret',
});

// Function to post a twoot
function postTweet() {
  const tweet = 'Hello, world! Automating Twitter
posts with Node.js! #Automation';
```

```
T.post('statuses/update', { status: tweet },
(err, data, response) => {
    if (err) {
      console.log('Error posting tweet:', err);
    } else {
      console.log('Tweet posted successfully:',
data.text);
    }
  });
}


// Schedule the tweet to be posted every day at
9 AM
cron.schedule('0 9 * * *', postTweet);   // Cron
expression for 9 AM daily
```

Explanation:

- **twit**: Used for interacting with the Twitter API to send posts and retrieve data.
- **cron.schedule('0 9 * * *')**: Schedules the postTweet function to run every day at **9 AM**.

By using **node-cron**, you can easily schedule tweets at different intervals without any manual intervention.

2. Automating Responses

You can also automate responses to specific events like mentions, direct messages, or comments. For instance, you might want to send an automated reply to anyone who mentions your account or asks a question.

Example: Automating Replies to Mentions

```javascript
const Twit = require('twit');

// Set up Twitter API credentials
const T = new Twit({
  consumer_key: 'your-api-key',
  consumer_secret: 'your-api-secret',
  access_token: 'your-access-token',
  access_token_secret:        'your-access-token-
secret',
});

// Function to reply to mentions
function replyToMentions() {
  const params = {
    q: '@yourTwitterHandle',   // Replace with
your Twitter handle
    count: 10,                 // Number of mentions
to check
```

```javascript
    result_type: 'recent',     // Fetch recent
mentions
  };

  T.get('search/tweets', params, (err, data,
response) => {
    if (err) {
      console.log('Error  fetching  mentions:',
err);
    } else {
      const mentions = data.statuses;
      mentions.forEach((mention) => {
        const user = mention.user.screen_name;
        const tweetId = mention.id_str;
        const replyText = `@${user} Thanks for
reaching out! How can we help?`;

        // Send a reply
        T.post('statuses/update',   {   status:
replyText,  in_reply_to_status_id:  tweetId  },
(err, data, response) => {
          if (err) {
            console.log('Error  sending  reply:',
err);
          } else {
            console.log('Replied to:', user);
          }
        });
      });
```

```
    }
  });
}
```

```
// Run the function every 10 minutes to check for
new mentions
setInterval(replyToMentions, 10 * 60 * 1000);
```

Explanation:

- **search/tweets**: Fetches recent mentions of your Twitter account.
- **in_reply_to_status_id**: Responds to the tweet by replying directly to the mention.
- **setInterval()**: Checks for new mentions every 10 minutes and automatically replies.

Real-World Example: Automating a Twitter Bot

Let's build a **Twitter bot** that not only posts tweets regularly but also replies to mentions, retweets content, and follows users who follow your account.

Example: Twitter Bot for Posting, Retweeting, and Following

1. **Install the necessary package**:

bash

```
npm install twit node-cron
```

2. **Set up the Twitter bot**:

javascript

```javascript
const Twit = require('twit');
const cron = require('node-cron');

// Set up Twitter API credentials
const T = new Twit({
  consumer_key: 'your-api-key',
  consumer_secret: 'your-api-secret',
  access_token: 'your-access-token',
  access_token_secret:        'your-access-token-
secret',
});

// Function to post a tweet
function postTweet() {
  const tweet = 'Hello, Twitter! Posting
regularly with my automation bot. #Automation
#Bot';
  T.post('statuses/update', { status: tweet },
(err, data, response) => {
    if (err) {
      console.log('Error posting tweet:', err);
    } else {
```

```
      console.log('Tweet posted successfully:',
data.text);
    }
  });
}


// Function to retweet the latest tweet with a
specific hashtag
function retweetHashtag() {
  const params = {
    q: '#AutomationBot',  // Look for tweets with
this hashtag
    result_type: 'recent',
    count: 1,
  };


  T.get('search/tweets', params, (err, data,
response) => {
    if (err) {
      console.log('Error   fetching   tweets:',
err);
    } else {
      const tweetId = data.statuses[0].id_str;
      T.post('statuses/retweet/:id',   {   id:
tweetId }, (err, data, response) => {
        if (err) {
          console.log('Error retweeting:', err);
        } else {
```

```
            console.log('Successfully
retweeted!');
          }
       });
     }
   });
}


// Function to follow back users who follow the
bot
function followBackUsers() {
  T.get('followers/list', { count: 10 }, (err,
data, response) => {
    if (err) {
      console.log('Error  fetching  followers:',
err);
    } else {
      data.users.forEach((user) => {
        T.post('friendships/create', { user_id:
user.id_str }, (err, data, response) => {
          if (err) {
            console.log('Error following user:',
err);
          } else {
            console.log(`Followed          back:
@${user.screen_name}`);
          }
        });
      });
```

```
    }
  });
}


// Schedule posts, retweets, and follow back
actions
cron.schedule('0 9 * * *', postTweet);  // Post
every day at 9 AM
cron.schedule('0 12 * * *', retweetHashtag);  //
Retweet hashtag every day at noon
cron.schedule('0 15 * * *', followBackUsers);  //
Follow back users every day at 3 PM
```

Explanation:

- **Post tweets**: Automatically posts tweets daily at 9 AM.
- **Retweet tweets**: Searches for recent tweets with the `#AutomationBot` hashtag and retweets them at noon daily.
- **Follow back users**: Checks for followers and follows them back at 3 PM every day.

This is a simple **Twitter bot** that automates several social media management tasks. You can expand it by adding more features, such as direct messaging users or tracking mentions of your brand.

Conclusion

In this chapter, we explored how to use **JavaScript** to automate social media management. We:

- Automated **social media posting** using the **Twitter API** and **node-cron** to schedule posts.
- Automated **responses to mentions** and automated actions like **retweeting** and **following back**.
- Built a **real-world Twitter bot** that posts tweets, retweets hashtags, and follows users automatically.

With these tools and techniques, you can save time, ensure consistent engagement, and improve the efficiency of your social media management tasks. JavaScript, combined with APIs like Twitter's, makes it easy to automate social media tasks without constant manual intervention.

CHAPTER 23

INTEGRATING JAVASCRIPT AUTOMATION WITH CLOUD SERVICES

Using AWS Lambda, Google Cloud Functions, or Azure Functions for Automation

Cloud services have revolutionized the way applications are built, deployed, and managed. **Serverless computing** services like **AWS Lambda**, **Google Cloud Functions**, and **Azure Functions** enable developers to run code in the cloud without managing servers, making them ideal for automating tasks that don't require a persistent server running 24/7.

Serverless platforms allow you to execute your JavaScript code in response to events like HTTP requests, file uploads, or scheduled tasks. These platforms automatically scale based on demand, making them cost-effective and efficient for running automation scripts.

1. AWS Lambda

AWS Lambda is Amazon's serverless compute service that allows you to run code without provisioning or managing servers. You can trigger Lambda functions using AWS services (like **S3**, **SNS**, or **API Gateway**) or external events.

- **Pricing**: You are charged based on the number of requests and the duration of the function execution (in milliseconds).
- **Languages Supported**: AWS Lambda supports several programming languages, including JavaScript (Node.js).

Example: Running a Simple AWS Lambda Function in JavaScript

1. **Set up your AWS Lambda Function**:
   - In the **AWS Management Console**, navigate to **Lambda** and create a new function.
   - Choose **Node.js** as the runtime environment.
2. **Example Code for a Simple Lambda Function**:

javascript

```javascript
exports.handler = async (event) => {
  // Log the event that triggered the function
  console.log('Event:',    JSON.stringify(event,
null, 2));
```

264

```
// Perform some action (e.g., return a message)
const message = 'Hello from AWS Lambda!';

// Return the result
return {
  statusCode: 200,
  body: JSON.stringify({ message: message }),
  };
};
```

Explanation:

- **exports.handler**: The entry point for the Lambda function. When triggered, this function is executed.
- **event**: Contains the event data that triggered the Lambda function (e.g., an S3 file upload or API request).

3. **Invoke the Lambda Function**:
   o The Lambda function can be triggered by an **AWS service** (like an HTTP request via **API Gateway**, or an S3 upload) or manually invoked.

2. Google Cloud Functions

Google Cloud Functions is a lightweight, serverless computing service that runs code in response to events. You can use it to handle HTTP requests, Cloud Pub/Sub messages, or file changes in **Google Cloud Storage**.

265

- **Pricing**: You are charged based on the number of invocations, execution time, and memory used.
- **Languages Supported**: JavaScript (Node.js), Python, Go, and more.

Example: Running a Google Cloud Function in JavaScript

1. **Create a Cloud Function**:
   o In the **Google Cloud Console**, go to **Cloud Functions** and create a new function.
   o Select **Node.js** as the runtime environment.
2. **Example Code for a Simple Google Cloud Function**:

javascript

```
const    functions    =    require('@google-
cloud/functions-framework');

// Create an HTTP Cloud Function
functions.http('helloWorld', (req, res) => {
  console.log('Request received:', req.body);
  res.status(200).send('Hello from Google Cloud
Functions!');
});
```

Explanation:

- **functions.http()**: Defines an HTTP function that handles HTTP requests and sends responses.

- **`req.body`**: Contains the body of the HTTP request.

3. **Deploy the Cloud Function**:
   - o Use the Google Cloud Console or the **gcloud CLI** to deploy the function. It can be triggered by an HTTP request or other events.

3. Azure Functions

Azure Functions is a serverless compute service provided by Microsoft Azure, allowing you to run JavaScript, C#, and other languages in response to events like HTTP requests, database updates, or timers.

- **Pricing**: Azure Functions are priced based on execution time, memory consumption, and the number of invocations.
- **Languages Supported**: JavaScript (Node.js), C#, Python, and more.

Example: Running a Simple Azure Function in JavaScript

1. **Create an Azure Function**:
   - o In the **Azure Portal**, create a new Function App and choose **JavaScript** as the language.
2. **Example Code for a Simple Azure Function**:

```javascript
```

```
module.exports = async function (context, req) {
  context.log('JavaScript HTTP trigger function
processed a request.');

  // Send a response
  context.res = {
    status: 200,
    body: 'Hello from Azure Functions!',
  };
};
```

Explanation:

- **`module.exports`**: Exports the function that is executed when the event (like an HTTP request) occurs.
- **`context.res`**: The response that is sent back after the function processes the request.

3. **Triggering the Azure Function**:
   o The function can be triggered by an HTTP request, a timer, or other Azure services (like an event in **Azure Blob Storage**).

Running JavaScript Automation in the Cloud

Cloud platforms such as **AWS Lambda**, **Google Cloud Functions**, and **Azure Functions** allow you to run your

268

JavaScript automation scripts without needing to maintain servers. These platforms handle the infrastructure, scaling, and resource management, letting you focus on writing the code.

Steps to Run Automation in the Cloud:

1. **Write the JavaScript automation script**.
2. **Deploy the script** to the respective cloud platform (AWS Lambda, Google Cloud Functions, or Azure Functions).
3. **Set up triggers** to execute the automation script (e.g., scheduled cron jobs, HTTP requests, file uploads).
4. **Monitor and scale** the function based on usage.

Real-World Example: Automating Cloud Resource Provisioning

A real-world use case is automating **cloud resource provisioning**. For instance, you might want to automatically spin up a new virtual machine (VM) or create cloud storage buckets based on incoming requests or specific conditions.

Example: Automating EC2 Instance Creation with AWS Lambda

In this example, we'll create an AWS Lambda function that automatically provisions an **EC2 instance** when triggered by an HTTP request. This is useful for automating infrastructure management, scaling resources on-demand, or automating other cloud services.

269

1. **Set Up IAM Role**:
   o Ensure your Lambda function has the necessary IAM role with **EC2** permissions (ec2:RunInstances).
2. **Example Lambda Function Code to Provision an EC2 Instance**:

javascript

```javascript
const AWS = require('aws-sdk');
const ec2 = new AWS.EC2();

exports.handler = async (event) => {
  const params = {
    ImageId: 'ami-0abcdef1234567890', // Replace with your AMI ID
    InstanceType: 't2.micro',
    MinCount: 1,
    MaxCount: 1,
    KeyName: 'your-ec2-keypair', // Replace with your EC2 key pair name
  };

  try {
    const result = await ec2.runInstances(params).promise();
    console.log('EC2 Instance created:', result);
    return {
```

```
      statusCode: 200,
      body:      JSON.stringify('EC2      instance
provisioned successfully'),
    };
  } catch (error) {
    console.error('Error      provisioning      EC2
instance:', error);
    return {
      statusCode: 500,
      body:   JSON.stringify('Error   provisioning
EC2 instance'),
    };
  }
};
```

Explanation:

- **AWS.EC2()**: Instantiates the EC2 service client.
- **ec2.runInstances()**: Launches a new EC2 instance based on the specified parameters (e.g., AMI ID, instance type).
- **await**: The function waits for the EC2 instance to be created before responding.

3. **Triggering the Lambda Function**:
    o The Lambda function can be triggered by an **API Gateway endpoint**, making it accessible via HTTP requests. You can also use other events

271

like **CloudWatch Events** or **S3** file uploads to trigger the provisioning process.

Conclusion

In this chapter, we explored how to integrate **JavaScript automation** with **cloud services** like **AWS Lambda**, **Google Cloud Functions**, and **Azure Functions**. We discussed:

- How to use **serverless functions** for automating tasks in the cloud, removing the need to manage servers.
- How to automate cloud resource provisioning, like creating EC2 instances using AWS Lambda.
- The benefits of **serverless computing**, including reduced management overhead, automatic scaling, and cost-effectiveness.

By integrating JavaScript with cloud platforms, you can automate infrastructure management, scale resources on-demand, and implement other cloud-based automation workflows efficiently. Serverless computing provides the flexibility and scalability needed for modern automation tasks.

CHAPTER 24

OPTIMIZING AUTOMATION SCRIPTS FOR PERFORMANCE

Improving the Performance of Automation Scripts

When writing automation scripts, especially those that run on a large scale or deal with heavy tasks like data processing, **performance optimization** is essential. Optimizing your automation scripts can lead to faster execution times, reduced resource usage, and a more reliable system. Here are key areas to focus on when optimizing automation scripts:

1. Minimize Synchronous Blocking Operations

JavaScript is single-threaded, and if you have synchronous operations in your script, they can block the event loop, slowing down your script and other concurrent tasks. To improve performance:

- Avoid using blocking functions like `fs.readFileSync()` or `http.getSync()`.

- Use asynchronous versions of I/O functions and make use of **Promises** or **async/await** to prevent blocking the event loop.

Example: Avoiding Synchronous File Operations

```javascript
const fs = require('fs');

// Synchronous (slow)
const                    dataSync                 =
fs.readFileSync('largeFile.txt');

// Asynchronous (faster)
fs.readFile('largeFile.txt', 'utf8', (err, data)
=> {
  if (err) throw err;
  console.log('Data:', data);
});
```

2. Minimize Memory Usage

If your automation script processes large amounts of data, it can quickly consume significant memory. To avoid running into memory bottlenecks, follow these tips:

- **Stream data**: Use streams for handling large files or datasets instead of loading them entirely into memory.

274

- **Garbage collection**: Ensure that you're not holding references to unnecessary objects. **null** or **delete** objects that are no longer needed to allow the garbage collector to free up memory.

Example: Using Streams to Process Large Files

javascript

```
const fs = require('fs');
const readline = require('readline');

// Stream reading a large file line by line to
minimize memory usage
const rl = readline.createInterface({
  input: fs.createReadStream('largeFile.txt'),
  output: process.stdout,
  terminal: false,
});

rl.on('line', (line) => {
  console.log('Processing line:', line); //
Process each line of the file
});
```

3. Optimize Data Structures

Efficient data structures help reduce memory usage and improve execution speed:

275

- Use **arrays** for ordered collections.
- Use **objects** (hash maps) for fast lookups, especially when you need to store and access large amounts of data.
- Use **sets** for unique values if the data doesn't have duplicates.

Example: Using Objects for Faster Lookup

```javascript
const users = [
  { id: 1, name: 'Alice' },
  { id: 2, name: 'Bob' },
  { id: 3, name: 'Charlie' },
];

// Optimized: Using an object for fast lookup by user ID
const usersLookup = users.reduce((acc, user) =>
{
  acc[user.id] = user;
  return acc;
}, {});

console.log(usersLookup[1]); // Fast lookup by user ID
```

4. Parallelize Tasks

If your automation script needs to handle multiple independent tasks (such as downloading files, processing data, or making API calls), you can **parallelize** them to improve performance. Using **Promise.all()**, **Worker Threads**, or **Node.js streams** helps perform multiple tasks concurrently, reducing execution time.

Example: Parallelizing API Calls

javascript

```javascript
const axios = require('axios');

// Parallel API calls using Promise.all
const fetchData = async () => {
  const urls = ['https://api1.com',
'https://api2.com', 'https://api3.com'];
  try {
    const responses = await
Promise.all(urls.map(url => axios.get(url)));
    console.log('All data fetched:', responses);
  } catch (error) {
    console.error('Error fetching data:',
error);
  }
};

fetchData();
```

277

Using Tools for Profiling and Optimizing JavaScript Code

To ensure that your optimization efforts are effective, you should profile and measure the performance of your code. There are several tools available for **profiling** and **benchmarking** JavaScript code to help you identify bottlenecks.

1. Chrome DevTools (Node.js)

If you're running your automation script using **Node.js**, you can take advantage of **Chrome DevTools** for profiling. You can use the `--inspect` flag to start your script and inspect it in Chrome.

1. Start the script in inspect mode:

    bash

    ```
    node    --inspect-brk=0.0.0.0:9229    your-
    script.js
    ```

2. Open **Chrome DevTools** by navigating to **chrome://inspect** in your Chrome browser and click on "Inspect" for your script.
3. Use the **Profiler** tab in Chrome DevTools to analyze CPU usage and find areas that need optimization.

278

2. Node.js Built-in Profiler

Node.js has a built-in profiler that you can use to generate CPU profiles and identify performance bottlenecks.

bash

```
node --prof your-script.js
```

This will generate a file called isolate-xxxx-v8.log. You can analyze this file with the **node --prof-process** command to get a human-readable profile.

bash

```
node --prof-process isolate-xxxx-v8.log > processed-profile.txt
```

3. Benchmarking with console.time and console.timeEnd

For simpler scripts, you can use console.time() and console.timeEnd() to measure execution time between specific sections of your code.

Example: Benchmarking a Function

javascript

```
console.time('Function Execution Time');
```

```
// Simulate a function that takes time to run
setTimeout(() => {
  console.timeEnd('Function Execution Time'); //
Logs the time taken
}, 1000);
```

4. Third-Party Libraries for Performance Analysis

Libraries such as **Benchmark.js** or **speed-measure-webpack-plugin** can help you benchmark specific pieces of code and track performance across different versions of your script.

- **Benchmark.js** allows you to benchmark individual functions and algorithms with a focus on accuracy and reliability.

Real-World Example: Speeding Up a Large-Scale Data Processing Task

Let's consider an example where we need to process a large CSV file with millions of rows. The script needs to read the file, parse each row, and perform calculations (e.g., summing up values) or transformations on the data. This process can be slow if done inefficiently.

1. Original Approach (Slow and Memory-Intensive)

In the original script, the entire file is read into memory at once, which can lead to high memory usage and slow performance for large files.

```javascript
const fs = require('fs');

const data = fs.readFileSync('largeData.csv',
'utf8'); // Read the entire file into memory
const rows = data.split('\n'); // Split data into
rows

let total = 0;
rows.forEach(row => {
  const fields = row.split(',');
  total += parseFloat(fields[2]); // Assuming
column 2 contains the numeric value
});

console.log('Total:', total);
```

Problems:

- **Memory consumption**: Loading the entire file into memory can cause memory overload.

- **Synchronous blocking**: The script reads the file synchronously, blocking the event loop.

2. Optimized Approach (Using Streams)

We can optimize this by **streaming the data** instead of reading it all at once. **Streams** allow us to process the file line-by-line, reducing memory usage and speeding up the script.

```javascript
const fs = require('fs');
const readline = require('readline');

let total = 0;

// Create a readable stream from the file
const rl = readline.createInterface({
  input: fs.createReadStream('largeData.csv'),
  output: process.stdout,
  terminal: false,
});

rl.on('line', (line) => {
  const fields = line.split(',');
  total += parseFloat(fields[2]); // Assuming
column 2 contains the numeric value
});
```

```
rl.on('close', () => {
  console.log('Total:', total);    // Processed
total after the stream finishes
});
```

Improvements:

- **Lower memory usage**: We no longer load the entire file into memory; instead, we process each line as it's read.
- **Non-blocking**: We're using streams, so the event loop is not blocked while reading the file.

3. Further Optimizations

We can further improve performance by:

- **Parallelizing I/O**: If the processing of each row is independent, consider using worker threads or **Promise.all()** to handle multiple tasks concurrently.
- **Optimized Data Structures**: If the data involves looking up specific records frequently, you can use hash maps or sets to speed up searches.

Conclusion

In this chapter, we discussed how to optimize **automation scripts for performance**. Key topics included:

- **Minimizing synchronous operations** and using asynchronous techniques to prevent blocking the event loop.
- **Efficient memory usage** through streaming data and using appropriate data structures.
- **Tools for profiling and benchmarking**, such as **Chrome DevTools**, **Node.js Profiler**, and **Benchmark.js**, to help identify performance bottlenecks.
- **A real-world example** of optimizing a large-scale data processing task by switching from a synchronous approach to a streaming approach, drastically improving both speed and memory efficiency.

By implementing these optimizations, you can ensure that your automation scripts run efficiently, even when dealing with large datasets or performing resource-intensive tasks.

CHAPTER 25

ADVANCED JAVASCRIPT AUTOMATION PATTERNS

Using Design Patterns for More Complex Automation Tasks

When working on complex automation scripts, it's crucial to use **design patterns** that help improve code structure, maintainability, and scalability. Design patterns are reusable solutions to common problems that arise in software development. In the context of automation scripts, design patterns can help you break down complex tasks into more manageable components and ensure that your code is efficient, flexible, and easy to maintain.

Here are some common design patterns used in automation tasks:

1. Factory Pattern

The **Factory Pattern** allows you to create objects without specifying the exact class of the object that will be created. It's particularly useful in automation tasks where you might need to create different types of objects or services dynamically.

Example: Using Factory Pattern for Different Task Handlers

Imagine you have an automation system that handles different types of data processing tasks (e.g., CSV processing, JSON processing). You can use the Factory Pattern to create the appropriate handler based on the task type.

```javascript
class CsvProcessor {
  process(data) {
    console.log('Processing CSV data:', data);
  }
}

class JsonProcessor {
  process(data) {
    console.log('Processing JSON data:', data);
  }
}

class ProcessorFactory {
  static createProcessor(type) {
    switch (type) {
      case 'csv':
        return new CsvProcessor();
      case 'json':
        return new JsonProcessor();
      default:
        throw new Error('Unknown processor type');
```

```
      }
   }
}
```

```
// Usage
const processorType = 'csv'; // This could be
dynamically determined
const                  processor              =
ProcessorFactory.createProcessor(processorType)
;
processor.process('some data');
```

Explanation:

- **ProcessorFactory**: Creates the appropriate data processor based on the input type.
- The factory allows you to abstract the object creation process, which simplifies extending the script to handle new data formats or processing types.

2. Observer Pattern

The **Observer Pattern** allows one object (the "subject") to notify other objects (the "observers") when a certain event occurs. This pattern is particularly useful in event-driven automation tasks, where actions need to be triggered by specific events.

Example: Using Observer Pattern for Event-Driven Automation

```javascript

class EventEmitter {
  constructor() {
    this.events = {};
  }

  on(event, listener) {
    if (!this.events[event]) {
      this.events[event] = [];
    }
    this.events[event].push(listener);
  }

  emit(event, data) {
    if (this.events[event]) {
      this.events[event].forEach(listener    =>
listener(data));
    }
  }
}

// Usage
const emitter = new EventEmitter();

// Observer 1: Listen for data processing event
emitter.on('dataProcessed', (data) => {
  console.log('Observer  1  received  processed
data:', data);
```

```
});
```

```
// Observer 2: Listen for data processing event
emitter.on('dataProcessed', (data) => {
  console.log('Observer 2 received processed
data:', data);
});
```

```
// Emit event after data processing
emitter.emit('dataProcessed', 'Processed data');
```

Explanation:

- **EventEmitter**: This class manages the events and the listeners (observers). It allows you to register listeners (`on()`) and emit events (`emit()`).
- This pattern is useful for automating tasks where different components need to respond to the same event, such as updating a UI or triggering further tasks.

3. Command Pattern

The **Command Pattern** is used to encapsulate requests as objects, which allows you to pass requests as parameters, queue them, and execute them at a later time. It's useful in automation for scheduling and executing tasks dynamically.

Example: Using Command Pattern for Task Automation

```javascript
javascript

class Task {
  constructor(name) {
    this.name = name;
  }

  execute() {
    console.log(`Executing task: ${this.name}`);
  }
}

class TaskQueue {
  constructor() {
    this.tasks = [];
  }

  addTask(task) {
    this.tasks.push(task);
  }

  executeTasks() {
    this.tasks.forEach(task => task.execute());
  }
}

// Usage
const task1 = new Task('Backup Data');
const task2 = new Task('Send Email');
```

```
const task3 = new Task('Generate Report');

const taskQueue = new TaskQueue();
taskQueue.addTask(task1);
taskQueue.addTask(task2);
taskQueue.addTask(task3);

taskQueue.executeTasks();
```

Explanation:

- **Task**: Represents a task with a name and an `execute()` method.
- **TaskQueue**: A queue that holds tasks and provides an `executeTasks()` method to run them.
- The **Command Pattern** allows you to queue tasks and execute them in a controlled manner, which is useful for scheduling and managing multiple automated tasks.

Modularizing Automation Scripts

As automation scripts grow in complexity, **modularizing** your code into smaller, reusable, and manageable parts becomes essential. Modularization improves maintainability, readability, and reusability, especially for large-scale automation systems.

1. Splitting Functions into Modules

In JavaScript, you can modularize your code by splitting it into separate files and using **require** (in Node.js) or **import** (in ES6) to bring in the necessary functionality.

Example: Modularizing the Code

Create a file dataProcessor.js for processing data:

javascript

```
// dataProcessor.js
function processData(data) {
  console.log('Processing data:', data);
}

module.exports = { processData };
```

Then, in your main automation script, you can import and use the function:

javascript

```
// main.js
const        {        processData        }        =
require('./dataProcessor');

const data = 'Some data to process';
```

```
processData(data);
```

Explanation:

- By modularizing, you create reusable and maintainable components. Each module can handle one aspect of the automation process (e.g., data processing, sending emails), and you can import them into your main script as needed.

2. Using Packages for Common Tasks

For common tasks like file handling, sending HTTP requests, or managing schedules, consider using existing **npm packages** to modularize your work. This not only saves development time but also ensures that the code is efficient and widely used.

Example: Using `node-cron` for Scheduling

```javascript
const cron = require('node-cron');

// Schedule a task to run every day at midnight
cron.schedule('0 0 * * *', () => {
  console.log('This task runs every day at midnight');
});
```

By modularizing common tasks, you can avoid reinventing the wheel and keep your codebase clean.

Real-World Example: Building a Multi-Step Workflow Automation

In this real-world example, we'll automate a multi-step process where:

1. Data is downloaded from an API.
2. The data is processed (e.g., cleaned and transformed).
3. The processed data is stored in a database.
4. A report is generated and sent via email.

We'll use modularization and design patterns to structure the automation script.

Step 1: Create Modules for Each Task

1. **Download Data** (`downloadData.js`):

javascript

```
const axios = require('axios');

async function downloadData(url) {
  try {
    const response = await axios.get(url);
    return response.data;
```

```
  } catch (error) {
    console.error('Error   downloading   data:',
error);
  }
}


module.exports = { downloadData };
```

2. **Process Data** (processData.js):

javascript

```
function processData(rawData) {
  return rawData.map(item => ({
    id: item.id,
    name: item.name.toUpperCase(),
  }));
}


module.exports = { processData };
```

3. **Save Data to Database** (saveData.js):

javascript

```
const mysql = require('mysql2');


const db = mysql.createConnection({
  host: 'localhost',
  user: 'root',
```

```
  password: 'password',
  database: 'automation_db',
});

function saveData(data) {
  data.forEach(item => {
    db.query('INSERT INTO processed_data (id,
name) VALUES (?, ?)', [item.id, item.name], (err,
result) => {
      if (err) console.error('Error saving
data:', err);
    });
  });
}

module.exports = { saveData };
```

4. **Send Email Report** (sendEmail.js):

```javascript
const nodemailer = require('nodemailer');

async function sendEmail(subject, body) {
  const transporter =
nodemailer.createTransport({
    service: 'gmail',
    auth: {
      user: 'your-email@gmail.com',
      pass: 'your-email-password',
```

```javascript
  },
});

const mailOptions = {
  from: 'your-email@gmail.com',
  to: 'recipient@example.com',
  subject,
  text: body,
};

try {
  await transporter.sendMail(mailOptions);
  console.log('Report sent!');
} catch (error) {
  console.error('Error    sending    email:',
error);
  }
}

module.exports = { sendEmail };
```
Step 2: Main Automation Script
```javascript
const    {    downloadData    }    =
require('./downloadData');
const { processData } = require('./processData');
const { saveData } = require('./saveData');
const { sendEmail } = require('./sendEmail');
```

```
async function runWorkflow() {
  const                    dataUrl                    =
'https://api.example.com/data';
  const rawData = await downloadData(dataUrl);
  const processedData = processData(rawData);
  saveData(processedData);
  sendEmail('Data Processed', 'The data has been
processed and saved.');
}


runWorkflow();
```

Explanation:

- **Modularization**: Each task (download, process, save, send) is encapsulated in a separate module.
- **Main Script**: The main script orchestrates the entire workflow by calling the functions from each module in sequence.

Conclusion

In this chapter, we explored **advanced JavaScript automation patterns** to handle complex tasks:

- **Design patterns** such as the **Factory, Observer**, and **Command patterns** help manage complex workflows.

- **Modularization** ensures your automation scripts are maintainable, reusable, and easier to manage.
- A **real-world example** demonstrated how to build a multi-step workflow automation using these principles.

By following these advanced patterns and techniques, you can create robust and scalable automation scripts that are easier to maintain and extend over time.

CHAPTER 26

AUTOMATING THE DEVELOPMENT PROCESS WITH JAVASCRIPT

Automating Development Workflows (Builds, Testing, Linting)

In modern development, **automation** plays a crucial role in improving the efficiency and consistency of the development process. Automating tasks such as **builds**, **testing**, and **linting** can save significant time, reduce human error, and ensure that all team members follow the same coding practices. These automations help in streamlining repetitive tasks and allow developers to focus more on writing code rather than managing workflows.

Here are key areas of the development process that can be automated:

1. Automating Builds

A **build process** involves compiling code, bundling it, and preparing it for deployment. Automating this process ensures that developers don't have to manually build the project every time they make changes.

300

Example: Automating Builds with npm Scripts

You can use **npm scripts** to automate the build process. For example, you can use **Webpack** or **Parcel** to bundle your JavaScript files and assets.

```json
json

{
  "scripts": {
    "build": "webpack --mode production",
    "dev":      "webpack-dev-server      --mode
development"
  }
}
```

Here, we define two scripts:

- **build**: Runs Webpack in production mode to bundle the application.
- **dev**: Starts the Webpack development server for local development.

2. Automating Testing

Testing is a crucial part of the development process to ensure the quality and functionality of your code. You can automate unit tests, integration tests, and end-to-end tests to run whenever changes are made.

Example: Automating Testing with Jest

You can use a testing framework like **Jest** to run tests automatically.

```json
{
  "scripts": {
    "test": "jest"
  }
}
```

Running the `npm test` command will automatically execute the tests in your project, ensuring that any changes don't break the existing functionality.

3. Automating Linting and Code Formatting

Linting is the process of analyzing code to find potential errors, enforce coding conventions, and ensure code quality. **Code formatting** ensures that code follows a consistent style. These tools can be automated to run whenever you save or commit code.

Example: Automating Linting and Formatting with ESLint and Prettier

ESLint and **Prettier** are two popular tools used for linting and formatting JavaScript code.

1. **ESLint**: Lints JavaScript code to enforce coding standards.
2. **Prettier**: Automatically formats JavaScript code according to a specific style guide.

Here's how you can integrate ESLint and Prettier into your development workflow:

Using Tools Like Babel, ESLint, and Prettier to Streamline Coding

1. Setting Up Babel

Babel is a JavaScript compiler that allows you to use the latest JavaScript features (such as ES6+ syntax) while ensuring compatibility with older environments (like older browsers).

1. **Install Babel**:

bash

```
npm install --save-dev @babel/core @babel/cli
@babel/preset-env
```

2. **Create a `.babelrc` configuration file**:

json

```
{
  "presets": ["@babel/preset-env"]
```

303

}

3. **Add a build script to run Babel**:

```json
json

{
  "scripts": {
    "build": "babel src --out-dir dist"
  }
}
```

Now, running `npm run build` will compile JavaScript files in the `src` folder into the `dist` folder, using the latest JavaScript syntax.

2. Setting Up ESLint

ESLint helps you catch potential errors in your code and ensures consistent style across the codebase.

1. **Install ESLint**:

```bash
bash

npm install --save-dev eslint
```

2. **Initialize ESLint**:

```bash
bash
```

```
npx eslint --init
```

Follow the prompts to configure ESLint for your project. You can choose coding standards such as **Airbnb**, **Google**, or configure your own.

3. **Run ESLint**:

```json
json

{
  "scripts": {
    "lint": "eslint src"
  }
}
```

Running `npm run lint` will analyze your code in the `src` folder and show any linting errors or warnings.

3. Setting Up Prettier

Prettier is an automatic code formatter that works alongside ESLint to ensure consistent code style and improve readability.

1. **Install Prettier**:

```bash
bash

npm install --save-dev prettier
```

2. **Configure Prettier** (optional, create a `.prettierrc` file):

json

```json
{
  "semi": true,
  "singleQuote": true,
  "trailingComma": "es5"
}
```

3. **Run Prettier**:

json

```json
{
  "scripts": {
    "format": "prettier --write src/**/*.js"
  }
}
```

Running `npm run format` will automatically format your JavaScript files to match the style you've defined in `.prettierrc`.

4. Integrating ESLint and Prettier

To avoid conflicts between ESLint and Prettier, you can use an ESLint plugin for Prettier to ensure that both tools work together.

1. **Install ESLint Prettier Plugin**:

```bash
npm install --save-dev eslint-config-prettier
eslint-plugin-prettier
```

2. **Configure ESLint to Use Prettier**:

```json
{
  "extends": ["eslint:recommended",
"plugin:prettier/recommended"]
}
```

This configuration tells ESLint to use Prettier for code formatting while disabling formatting rules in ESLint that might conflict with Prettier.

Real-World Example: Automating Code Formatting and Linting for a Team Project

In a team project, automating code formatting and linting ensures that all developers follow the same coding standards, preventing unnecessary merge conflicts and promoting consistency across the codebase.

1. Setting Up the Development Environment

In a real-world team project, you would typically configure the automation tasks like linting and formatting in your `package.json` file:

json

```json
{
  "name": "team-project",
  "version": "1.0.0",
  "scripts": {
    "build": "webpack --mode production",
    "dev":      "webpack-dev-server       --mode development",
    "lint": "eslint src --fix",
    "test": "jest",
    "format": "prettier --write src/**/*.js"
  },
  "devDependencies": {
    "@babel/core": "^7.14.0",
    "@babel/preset-env": "^7.14.0",
    "babel-loader": "^8.2.2",
    "eslint": "^7.28.0",
    "eslint-config-prettier": "^8.3.0",
    "eslint-plugin-prettier": "^3.4.0",
    "jest": "^27.0.6",
    "prettier": "^2.3.2",
    "webpack": "^5.46.0",
```

```
    "webpack-cli": "^4.7.2",
    "webpack-dev-server": "^4.0.0"
  }
}
```

2. Enforcing Consistent Code Style in the Team

With the above configuration, your team can follow a streamlined workflow:

- **Linting**: Run `npm run lint` before committing code to ensure all code is following the defined style and free of errors.
- **Code Formatting**: Run `npm run format` to auto-format code and ensure consistent style across the codebase.
- **Building and Testing**: Use `npm run build` to automate the build process and `npm test` to run automated tests after every change.

3. Setting Up Pre-Commit Hooks with `husky`

To further automate the process and prevent poor code from being committed, you can use **Husky** to set up pre-commit hooks. This ensures that linting and formatting checks are run before code is committed to the repository.

1. **Install Husky**:

bash

```
npm install --save-dev husky
```

2. **Set Up Husky to Run Linting and Formatting on Pre-Commit**:

bash

```
npx husky-init && npm install
```

3. **Configure Pre-Commit Hook**:

bash

```
npx husky set .husky/pre-commit "npm run lint &&
npm run format"
```

With this setup, every time a developer tries to commit changes, **Husky** will automatically run `npm run lint` and `npm run format`. If the code doesn't pass linting or formatting checks, the commit will be blocked.

Conclusion

In this chapter, we covered how to automate various aspects of the **development process** using **JavaScript**:

310

- We discussed how to automate **builds**, **testing**, and **linting** using **npm scripts**, **ESLint**, **Prettier**, and **Babel**.
- We learned how to integrate tools like **ESLint** and **Prettier** to enforce coding standards and ensure that all team members follow the same guidelines.
- A **real-world example** demonstrated how to automate code formatting and linting in a team project, ensuring consistency and reducing the risk of errors.

By automating these tasks, you can improve the efficiency of your development workflow, maintain consistent code quality, and reduce the overhead associated with manual processes.

CHAPTER 27

SCALING AUTOMATION FOR LARGER PROJECTS

Best Practices for Scaling Automation in Large Systems

When working with large-scale systems, automation becomes increasingly important to ensure that tasks are consistently executed, environments are maintained, and systems are scaled efficiently. As projects grow in complexity, the automation strategy must evolve to handle higher levels of complexity, increased traffic, and more distributed systems. Here are some **best practices** for scaling automation in larger systems:

1. Break Automation Tasks into Smaller, Modular Units

In large projects, trying to handle everything in a single script can lead to complexity and hard-to-maintain code. To scale automation, break down your tasks into smaller, **modular units** that each handle a specific responsibility. For example:

- **Build automation**: Use specialized scripts for building different parts of the application (frontend, backend, services).

- **Deployment automation**: Break down the deployment pipeline into smaller steps (e.g., deployment to staging, then production, with quality checks in between).
- **Monitoring automation**: Set up independent monitoring and alerting for each part of the system.

By breaking down the tasks into smaller units, you can more easily manage and scale them as the system grows.

2. Use Distributed Task Queues

For large systems, a single server or service might not be sufficient to handle the load. In these cases, use **distributed task queues** (e.g., **RabbitMQ**, **Amazon SQS**, **Redis Queue**) to manage and distribute tasks across multiple workers. This allows you to scale tasks horizontally by adding more worker instances to process tasks concurrently.

- **Distributed task queues** are especially useful for background jobs like data processing, file uploads, email sending, and other tasks that are resource-intensive.

3. Use CI/CD Pipelines for Automation

In large systems, **Continuous Integration (CI)** and **Continuous Deployment (CD)** pipelines become essential for ensuring that new changes are automatically tested, built, and deployed to various environments (e.g., dev, staging, production).

Automate your entire deployment process, from code merging to testing, building, and deployment. Using tools like **Jenkins**, **GitLab CI**, **CircleCI**, and **GitHub Actions** can help automate your workflows.

4. Automate Configuration Management

As systems grow, configuration management becomes more challenging. Automating the management of **configuration files**, **environments**, and **variables** is essential to ensure consistency across development, staging, and production environments. You can use tools like:

- **Docker** for containerized environments.
- **Kubernetes** for orchestrating containers.
- **Ansible**, **Chef**, or **Puppet** for infrastructure automation.

5. Monitor and Test Automation at Scale

Automation tests should also be automated and scaled. For large systems, use:

- **Automated performance testing**: Ensure that scaling doesn't degrade performance using tools like **JMeter** or **Artillery**.
- **Automated load testing**: Test how your automated deployment process behaves under load.

- **Automated health checks**: Ensure that services are running and healthy using tools like **Prometheus** or **Datadog**.

Managing Dependencies and Automating Dependency Management

In larger projects, managing and automating **dependencies** becomes critical. Here are some strategies for ensuring your dependencies are efficiently managed:

1. Automate Dependency Updates

Keeping dependencies up-to-date is crucial in large projects to avoid vulnerabilities, ensure compatibility, and take advantage of performance improvements in newer versions. Automate dependency updates by using tools like:

- **Dependabot**: GitHub's built-in tool that automatically creates pull requests when dependencies need updating.
- **Renovate**: An open-source tool that automates dependency management by creating pull requests for dependency updates.

Example: Automating Dependency Updates with Dependabot

1. Enable Dependabot in your GitHub repository.

2. Dependabot will automatically create pull requests when new versions of your dependencies are released, keeping your project up to date.

2. Use Package Managers Efficiently

Automating the installation and management of dependencies is essential for scaling your development process. Use modern package managers like **npm**, **yarn**, or **pnpm** to ensure consistency across environments and improve dependency resolution.

- **Lockfiles**: Always use `package-lock.json` (for npm) or `yarn.lock` (for Yarn) to lock dependency versions.
- **Automated Package Audits**: Use tools like **npm audit** or **yarn audit** to automatically check for vulnerabilities in your dependencies.

Example: Automating Package Audits

You can run automated security audits as part of your CI/CD pipeline to ensure that no insecure packages are introduced.

```json
{
  "scripts": {
    "audit": "npm audit"
  }
}
```

You can run `npm run audit` as part of your build or pre-deployment process to check for vulnerabilities.

3. Version Control for Dependencies

Use **semantic versioning** (semver) to ensure that dependencies are compatible with your system. By following semantic versioning (e.g., `1.2.3`), you can automate the process of upgrading to new versions that are backward-compatible while avoiding breaking changes.

4. Containerization to Manage Dependencies

When automating large-scale systems, consider using **Docker** to containerize your application and its dependencies. Docker allows you to package the application along with all required dependencies into a container, ensuring that your automation scripts work in any environment consistently.

Real-World Example: Automating the Deployment of a Microservices Architecture

In a microservices architecture, managing multiple services, databases, and networking configurations can quickly become complex. Automating the deployment of such an architecture requires careful orchestration and the use of modern tools to manage the deployment of each individual service.

317

Example: Automating Microservices Deployment with Docker and Kubernetes

1. Containerizing Each Service with Docker

Each microservice can be packaged into a Docker container. Here's an example `Dockerfile` for a Node.js service:

dockerfile

```
# Dockerfile for Node.js Service
FROM node:14

WORKDIR /app

 package.json package-lock.json ./
RUN npm install


 . .


EXPOSE 3000

CMD ["node", "index.js"]
```

Each microservice would have a similar Dockerfile, which ensures that the service is packaged with all necessary dependencies and can run anywhere with Docker installed.

2. Using Kubernetes for Orchestration

318

Once the services are containerized, you can automate their deployment using **Kubernetes**. Here's an example **Kubernetes Deployment** YAML file for deploying a microservice:

yaml

```yaml
apiVersion: apps/v1
kind: Deployment
metadata:
  name: my-microservice
spec:
  replicas: 3  # Scale to 3 instances
  selector:
    matchLabels:
      app: my-microservice
  template:
    metadata:
      labels:
        app: my-microservice
    spec:
      containers:
      - name: my-microservice
        image: my-microservice:latest
        ports:
        - containerPort: 3000
```

This YAML file defines how Kubernetes should deploy and scale the service, manage replicas, and expose the service.

319

3. Automating the Deployment Process with CI/CD

To automate the deployment of the entire microservices architecture, you can integrate Docker and Kubernetes with a **CI/CD pipeline**. This pipeline can be set up with tools like **Jenkins**, **GitLab CI**, or **GitHub Actions**.

Example: Using GitHub Actions for CI/CD

Here's a sample GitHub Actions workflow for deploying a microservices application:

```yaml
name: Deploy Microservices

on:
  push:
    branches:
      - main

jobs:
  build:
    runs-on: ubuntu-latest

    steps:
    - name: Checkout repository
      uses: actions/checkout@v2
```

```
      - name: Set up Docker
        uses: docker/setup-buildx-action@v1

      - name: Build Docker images
        run: |
          docker    build    -t    my-microservice
./service1
          docker    build    -t    my-microservice
./service2

      - name: Push Docker images to Docker Hub
        run: |
          docker push my-microservice:latest

      - name: Deploy to Kubernetes
        run: |
          kubectl apply -f k8s/deployment.yaml
```

Explanation:

- The workflow is triggered by a **push** to the `main` branch.
- **Docker images** for each microservice are built and pushed to **Docker Hub**.
- **Kubernetes deployment** is updated automatically using `kubectl apply`.

4. **Monitoring and Scaling**

After the services are deployed, you can use Kubernetes' built-in monitoring tools (like **Prometheus** and **Grafana**) to track the performance of each service and scale them automatically based on demand.

Conclusion

In this chapter, we explored how to **scale automation** for large systems, especially in complex microservices architectures:

- We covered **best practices for scaling automation**, such as breaking tasks into smaller units, using distributed task queues, and implementing CI/CD pipelines.
- We discussed **managing dependencies** and automating dependency management to ensure that the system is kept up-to-date and secure.
- A **real-world example** demonstrated how to automate the deployment of a **microservices architecture** using **Docker, Kubernetes**, and **GitHub Actions**.

By following these practices and leveraging powerful tools, you can automate and scale your workflows efficiently, ensuring the smooth deployment and management of complex systems.

www.ingramcontent.com/pod-product-compliance
Lightning Source LLC
LaVergne TN
LVHW051431050326
832903LV00030BD/3026